Maxine Smith
from Natalie

# England

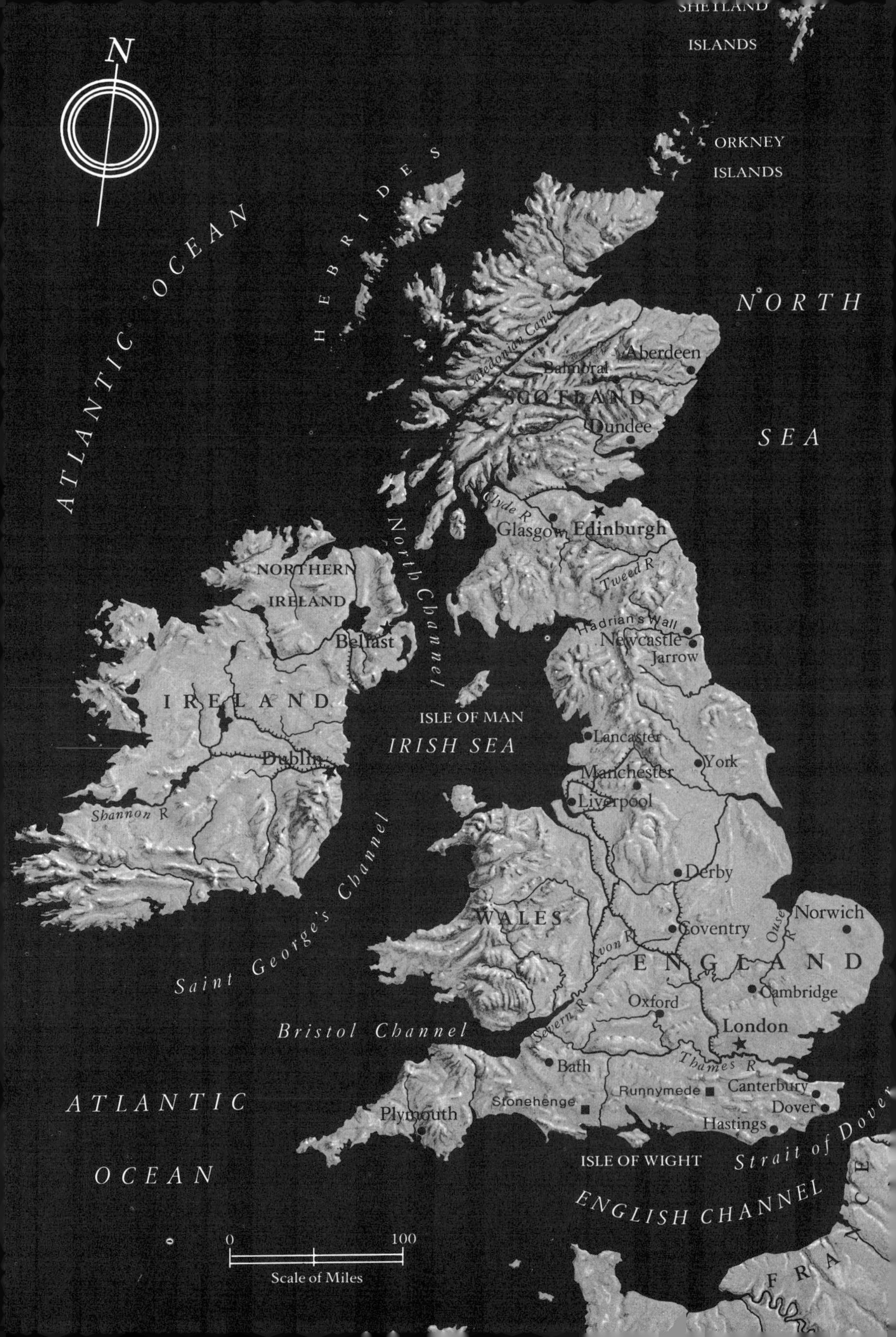
N
SHETLAND
ISLANDS
ORKNEY
ISLANDS
HEBRIDES
ATLANTIC OCEAN
NORTH
SEA
Caledonian Canal
Aberdeen
Balmoral
SCOTLAND
Dundee
Clyde R
Glasgow
Edinburgh
Tweed R
North Channel
NORTHERN
IRELAND
Belfast
Hadrian's Wall
Newcastle
Jarrow
IRELAND
ISLE OF MAN
IRISH SEA
Lancaster
York
Dublin
Manchester
Liverpool
Shannon R
Saint George's Channel
Derby
WALES
Norwich
Ouse R
Coventry
Avon R
ENGLAND
Cambridge
Oxford
Severn R
Bristol Channel
London
Thames R
Bath
Runnymede
Canterbury
Stonehenge
Dover
Plymouth
Hastings
ATLANTIC
OCEAN
ISLE OF WIGHT
Strait of Dover
ENGLISH CHANNEL
FRANCE
0
100
Scale of Miles

THE HORIZON CONCISE HISTORY OF

# England

by R. J. White

Published by
AMERICAN HERITAGE PUBLISHING CO., INC.
New York 1971

Investiture of Prince Charles–United Press International; Helmet of the Royal House Horse Guards–Robert Abels, Inc., New York; Map by Henry Le Roy, 1639–H.P. Kraus, New York; William Shakespeare–Collection of Bradley Bransford; London policeman's badge–Arie de Zanger; Miniature of Mary Queen of Scots, 1813–A La Vieille Russie, Inc.; Rolls Royce symbol–Arie de Zanger; English blunderbuss, c. 1790 – Rea & Sons, New York; William III, needlework, c. 1694–1702–Ginsburg & Levy, New York


Library of Congress Catalog Card Number: 79-149733
ISBN: 07-069690-X

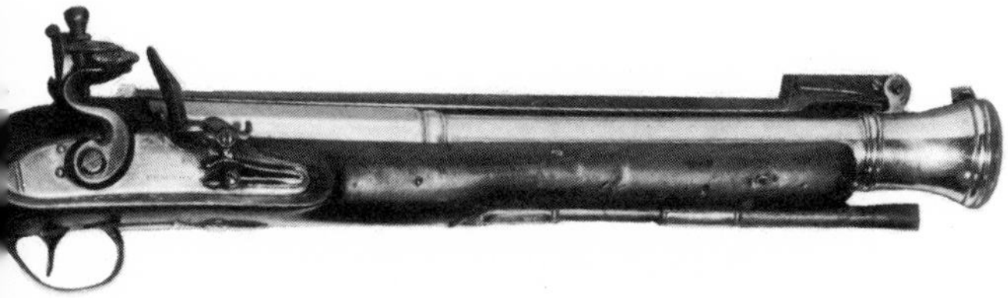

CHAPTER I

# THE ISLAND AND ITS INVADERS

English history concerns a people who first settled an island off the coast of continental Europe and went on to govern a considerable portion of the habitable globe. Refugees from the mainland, they were from the beginning a mixed lot, and their story is a standing refutation of all theories that claim racial purity to be a recipe for national success.

No one knows when the land bridge between Dover and Calais became flooded, but for thousands of years in the remote past the island was part of the mainland, and across that low, connective, tidewater plain came the primitive hunters of Europe, following the last northward retreat of the ice sheet in pursuit of the mammoth and reindeer. Even after the sea moved into the valley, carving its verdant slopes into distinctive chalk cliffs and creating a moat between island and mainland, families and whole tribes of people continued to make the crossing, coming in boats no bigger than dugout canoes and wicker coracles, setting a pattern of tribal invasion that was to continue until the Norman Conquest. These first accidental settlers were followed by groups of warriors migrating from what is now France, Germany, Holland, and Scandinavia, who came up the inviting estuaries into

*Stonehenge, the most celebrated monument surviving from pre-Roman England*

the fertile lowlands of south and east, and then shoved back the earlier inhabitants toward the more mountainous north and west. After some tens of centuries of this, ending with the last successful invasion of the island in A.D. 1066, physical insularity would become one of the dominating facts of English history, often of greater psychological than material import, but a fact, nonetheless, that created in the minds of the people a strong sense of security and invincibility, and—some thought—an assumption of superiority.

As on the Continent, the prehistoric period of the land stretches for countless millenniums back into impenetrable mists of time, while the natives gradually found their way, by slow and arduous stages, toward the beginnings of a civilized way of life. Several thousands of years before our era, certain of the island's inhabitants undertook the extraordinary construction known as Stonehenge in Wiltshire, not far from Salisbury, probably to serve ritual purposes. It remains the most majestic and enduring of ancient British monuments, a testimony to herculean efforts and primitive engineering skills.

The Bronze Age was followed by a succession of Iron Ages, during which Britain derived its name from the fair-haired, Brythonic-speaking Celts who came there from across the Channel. The south and east of the island is still studded with their hill-forts, some of which now appear like mere natural eminences, others of which still tower over the landscape majestically, like Maiden Castle in Dorset. Some of these Celtic "displaced persons," looking for allies to save them from everlasting internecine warfare, summoned to their aid the Roman commander, Julius Caesar, from his camp in Gaul. Caesar made two expeditions to the island in 55 and 54 B.C., and with these first recorded invasions of the land the history of England—as it was to be called—really began.

"The island is triangular," Caesar wrote in his campaign memoirs called *De Bello Gallico* (*The Gallic Wars*), "one of its sides facing Gaul." Its strategic location, in addition to its economic resources of iron and tin, silver and lead, and rumors of pearl fisheries, aroused Rome's interest, and because the fierce, woad-painted inhabitants were often in league with Rome's Continental rebels and enemies, the offshore island simply had to be brought under Roman dominion. The task was hard and repellent to the legionaries who undertook it, for the Romans seem to have regarded this island adjoining Ultima Thule as the vestibule of Hades, a region of mists and half-light where the ghosts of the dead floated about crying with the weird voices of sea birds.

Nevertheless, in A.D. 43 the emperor Claudius undertook the actual conquest of England, and it was then that the Romans brought the island into the known world, mining its various metals and cultivating its abundant corn. They subdued at least its southernmost inhabitants and introduced a form of urban- and villa-centered living, which, however, was to be abandoned after the legions departed to defend Rome itself from the onslaught of Alaric and the Goths in A.D. 410. The Romans ruled the Romano-British island for a period as long as that which separates the present time from the reign of Queen Elizabeth I. During those nearly four centuries they brought to it the city, the forum, the theater, the colonnaded marketplace, the country house, or villa, the central-heating system, the cabbage, the onion, the rose, the beech tree and the sweet chestnut, a wonderful system of roads, a postal system, public baths, and an official language spoken and written in most of the world.

As long as the Romans were there, it was not assumed that dirtiness was next to godliness; that proximation took root in the Christian Middle Ages, when it was said that baths, especially public ones with their mixed bathing, encouraged immorality. Not until the twentieth century, with the setting-in of the "little ice age," did the people of the island return to central heating, ridding themselves of the ancient British idea that there is something degenerate and even immoral about feeling comfortable. It may not be altogether fortuitous that northerners still suspect the people of the southern counties (where the Romans ruled) of being what they call "nesh," which means "soft." It has been seriously maintained that the softness inculcated in the people under Roman rule made them an easy prey to the Germanic invaders who began to infiltrate the island from more virile lands like Jutland and Schleswig as the legions withdrew.

The Britons whom the Romans finally subdued were a fearsome folk. Not only did they paint themselves blue. They drove war chariots armed at the axles with scythes. Their religion was that of the druids, and although we know little of its rites and ritual we do know that it entailed human sacrifice. The Romans had scant respect for human life, as we can tell from their gladiatorial shows, but they drew the line at sacrificing humans to propitiate the gods. They undertook a massive campaign to stamp out druidism, which also had economic and political affiliations inimical to imperial interests. Suetonius Paulinus, a veteran soldier of the North African campaign, achieved the destruction of druidical religion. From Suetonius' bitter war of suppression emerged the first historical British heroine—Boadicea, queen of the Iceni, a rebellious people centered in Camulodunum, the modern Colchester, a town where Roman relics still peep through the later accretions of the Gothic centuries. (Few places in

*Hadrian's Wall marked the northern boundary of Roman Britain.*

the island afford more striking evidences of the mixed elements that make up the history of England.) As a resistance leader, the "British Queen" gave the Roman conquerors a good run for their money. She and her followers delivered some notable cities to the flames and slaughtered thousands of Romanizing Britons before she took her own life after being captured by the legionaries, whom the Iceni had long terrified with their wild flowing hair, their hideous war cries, and their scythed chariots. It is said that Boadicea and her furies might have eluded their fate longer had their retreat not been hampered by traffic jams brought about by wagonloads of female sightseers who had come to see the hoped-for triumph of their queen, much as the ladies of Washington, D.C., turned out in their carriages for the first battle of Bull Run. Boadicea should be memorialized by

a cenotaph in the Suffolk countryside where she and her daughters died. Instead, the Victorians, always appreciative of lost causes and "small nations struggling to be free," put up a handsome bronze representation of the queen driving her chariot behind prancing steeds close to the Houses of Parliament on the Thames embankment.

Britain became formally Christian with the emperor Constantine's conversion and concordat with the Roman Church in A.D. 313. Constantine was hailed as emperor at York, and the people of the island have liked to believe that his mother, Helena, was a Romano-British woman. (The first Christian emperor was greatly attached to his mother; she was to become the notable saint accredited with having discovered the True Cross during her travels in Palestine.)

As if it was not sufficient honor to have had the earliest Christian emperor hailed on their soil and his family connected with the legionary city of Colchester, the Romano-British produced in the lay monk Pelagius the first British heretic. For Pelagius courageously denied the double-dyed doctrine of original sin upheld by Saint Augustine, the famous bishop of Hippo—author of the *City of God*—and taught rather that men may be saved by their natural goodness and their own efforts. In outward aspect Pelagius seems to have resembled that well-known caricature of the Englishman, Colonel Blimp, or Bernard Shaw's Britannus in *Caesar and Cleopatra:* friends of his great enemy Saint Augustine described him as "bull-necked, full-faced, broad-shouldered, corpulent, and slow-moving, like a tortoise weighed down with porridge." However, in the perspective of more than fifteen centuries of British history, the Christian experience of the people of the island has never quite lost the optimistic streak given to it by Pelagius and Pelagianism.

It was once believed that when the Roman legions withdrew from Britain, the Germanic invasions followed like a cataclysm, a swift and overwhelming flood. In fact, the Germanic tribes conquered here, as elsewhere, by infiltration. They came from Schleswig, Frisia, and North German lands at the mouth of the Elbe, and the most notable among them were the Saxons, who, tradition has it, took their tribal name from "seaxan," the Old English word for "knife." The Angles were named after Angeln, a district of Schleswig, and the Jutes took their name from Jutland. For long enough Rome had organized the

*A detail from a medieval French tapestry characteristically identifies King Arthur by three crowns on his gown and pennant.*

defense of the British coasts under an official who bore the title of Count of the Saxon Shore. The Classis Britannica, or British fleet, was based at Boulogne opposite the coasts of Kent and Sussex, and there was a fine system of signal stations along the coast of Yorkshire to warn of approaching trouble. But many of the conquering Germans had been taken on as auxiliaries of the Roman forces, and such servants often became masters. By A.D. 500, Angles, Saxons, and Jutes physically controlled about a quarter of the British Isles. In the southwest the invasion was stemmed by a Romano-British victory at Mount Badon, and although we do not know exactly where this place was, it is here that we catch a glimpse of the celebrated character known as King Arthur. That romantic figure of British literature and romance claims his shadowy role in history as one of the saviors of a harassed people in the sub-Roman period, a truly Dark Age lasting for about two hundred years. Arthur is no more and no less historically established than Robin Hood, hardly more so than the Scarlet Pimpernel—and no less beloved than both. Although the Romano-Britons continued to resist the Germans, their land was finally overwhelmed. Out of this chaotic period emerges Saxon England (and we can at last legitimately use the term "England"); here English history, properly so-called, had a fresh beginning.

The conquerors were bloody-minded pirates intent on destroying a higher civilization than their own, but they were also settlers who had come to till the soil. They penetrated into the island by the waterways, avoiding the Romano-British sites and planting their homesteads by the rivers rather than by the roads. As their descendants were also to be, they were a warlike but not a military folk. The nineteenth-century English liked to imagine that these were a freedom-loving people, progenitors of democracy and liberty (which were somehow thought to be closely related), in the composite which made up the English. They were further imagined to have governed themselves through popular assemblies gathered under the greenwood tree. The local militia, or *fyrd,* was in fact made up of freemen, all of whom were obliged to serve in it. But "Anglo-Saxon democracy" was a myth; stalwart freemen were the exception rather than the rule in that slave-ridden society. What could be expected of heathen tribes carving up a conquered land? As the historian George M. Trevelyan wrote: "Primitive societies, if they are ever to move on towards knowledge, wealth, and ordered freedom, are obliged to travel in the first instance not along the path of democratic equality but along the path of aristocracy, kingship, and priesthood." If there was equality in Anglo-Saxon England, it was the equality of poverty and ignorance. Advance to any higher level of civilization could only be through the emergence of inequality and privilege on the part of the few. Kingship, aristocracy, priesthood—in short, feudalism—have been called a "natural and even a necessary stage" in English history. In certain respects the life of the pioneer in Saxon England resembled that of his later counterpart in the wilderness of America: the forest had to be cleared to make even the most rudimentary agriculture possible; a dwelling had to be constructed; and a man had to have a weapon at hand even while he used the axe and plow. At first, neighbors were few and remote; then tiny settlements were established, and since the normal conditions of life during the Saxon period were invasion and bloodshed, it was inevitable that the folk in these early communities should devise a means of self-protection. Feudalism was just such a method: differentiating between the roles of soldier and husbandman made it possible to safeguard the helpless, to conduct war, to settle outlying lands, and to till the soil. Given the barbarian conquests as an unalterable fact, feudalism meant civilization.

Once again it was from Rome that the new seeds of civilization were sown—this time by a handful of Italian monks sent among the pagan Saxons by Pope Gregory the Great in 597 to bring about the reconversion of the island. There is a cherished tradition among the English that the pope was inspired to promote this great work by the sight of fair-haired English boys being sold in the slave market at Rome, where he made up his mind to transform the "Angles" into "Angels." Whatever the initial cause, another Saint Augustine (a later namesake of the bishop of Hippo), who became the first archbishop of Canterbury, and his missionary fellows were responsible for turning the heathen toward Christianity and bringing England in contact once more with the Mediterranean world. Monasteries sprang up across the land and there followed a golden age of Anglo-Saxon art and learning. From the Mediterranean came Latin and Greek scholars, bringing with them a store of books so rare as to be virtually unknown in England. Canterbury became a school, so did Jarrow and York; and with the Roman influence came the spread of church music and ecclesiastical architecture. Learning began to light up Britain's dark forests, which the Roman legionaries had never penetrated. Stone abbeys built by Benedictine monks housed increasing numbers of illuminated manuscripts and parchments. Inside monastery walls were libraries and scriptoria, where the painstaking work of copying manuscripts from the ancient world bore testimony to the *Opus Dei;* outside were the carefully cultivated gardens and herbs. Britain's art, which had its roots in barbaric forms and which had been influenced by the Celtic genius for curve and color, found new expression and a new range of subject matter in Christianity. Masterpieces such as the Lindisfarne Gospels and the sculptured crosses of northern England were the product of hands touched with genius and inspired by visions of a heavenly paradise. Soon the Christianized English were sending missionaries of their own to convert their Continental kinfolk in northern Europe. Early in the eighth century the great Anglo-Saxon epic *Beowulf* made its appearance. In Europe the most popular writer of his day was an English student of the classics, the abbot Aldhelm of Malmesbury. In 731 that extraordinary figure known to later generations as the Venerable Bede, the first English historian, who was universally acknowledged as the greatest scholar of his time, wrote his *Ecclesiastical History of the English People.* (To the influence of Bede the world also owes the practice, later adopted, of reckoning the years from the birth of Christ.) About 781 the Saxon monk Alcuin of York carried English learning to the court of Charlemagne, to inspire the Carolingian renaissance. Not for another thousand years, not until the century of the French Revolution, would England's influence on the continent of Europe be so deep or so enduring.

As the Celtic twilight had produced King Arthur, the emergent sunshine of the Saxons produced King Alfred, "England's darling." The finest flower of the early English state, he comes down to us as a great war leader in the English contest against the Danes, but he was much other and more than that. Alfred (*r.* 871–899) is the only English king to be known as "the Great," and the unique title was well deserved. Anyone who has seen his statue looking down the main street of Winchester, the ancient capital of Wessex (and therefore

*The art of manuscript illumination flourished in early England and also in Ireland, as shown by a leaf from the Book of Kells, about* A.D. *800.*

*An animal standard from a ninth-century Viking ship*

of England) will understand why. Like his near-contemporary Charlemagne, he was a mixture of soldier, scholar, and judge, whose dearest wish was that "all the youth now in England, born of freemen, who have the means they can apply to it" should be devoted to learning. He planned the education of his nobility and churchmen, much as Charlemagne had done and as Peter the Great of Russia was to do. He translated into English the *Pastoral Care* of Pope Gregory the Great, with an introduction lamenting the decline of learning in his time. It grieved him, he said, "to think that Englishmen who sought the things of the mind must now seek them abroad, when once men had come to England in search of learning and wisdom." This was sadly true, for by King Alfred's day the brief flourishing of Saxon learning that began with Saint Augustine was over. The monasteries, the centers of culture, had been destroyed by the latest wave of invaders—the Vikings, or Danes as they are commonly called in English history—who were threatening Alfred's kingdom as well.

Only in recent times have the English come to appreciate the European stature of their ancestors in the Saxon centuries. The name of Alfred the Great once awakened memories only of the refugee king hiding from his enemies in the marshes of Athelney. The embodiment of the hero-king, his story was the stuff of myth and legend, very much as King Arthur embodied the legend of the conquered Britons after the departure of the Roman legions. The hagiology produced by the much-conquered island of the early centuries struck their descendants as strange, picturesque, and even childish in later ages when conquest had become rather the lot of less fortunate peoples.

The fact remains that King Alfred was the organizer of victory in the English contest with the first Viking invasion. He improvised a navy; he set up a chain of *burghs,* or urban centers of defense, from Chester to Saint Albans. He led the national *fyrd,* consisting of all freemen in arms, at the battle of Edington, where he defeated the Danes and assured the independence of Wessex. Then, having fought the Danes, Alfred came to terms with them: he secured the conversion and baptism of the Danish king Guthrum, even as he treated with him for the division of England. The northeast, which was to be ruled by the Danes, became known as the Danelaw. The rest of the country, including what remained of seven kingdoms known as the Heptarchy, was to be ruled by the royal house of Wessex, Alfred's house. His domain became the embryo of a united England; from Wessex Alfred's son, daughter, and grandson eventually regained even the Danelaw, to become the first true rulers of England. But, starting in the late tenth century new Danish invaders overcame Alfred's successors. By 1017 Canute of Denmark ruled all England, peacefully and well; he also became king of Denmark and Norway, reigning over three countries until his death.

For their parts, the warlike, seafaring Danes, sharing the island with the Saxons, supplied the last and in some ways the most virile element in England's racial mixture. Among their many endeavors, the Danes further organized many of Saxon England's towns under the Danelaw, making them more efficient units. The Danes' so-called five boroughs—Derby, Leicester, Lincoln, Nottingham, and Stamford—were all military garrisons that developed into trading centers, each retaining its protective palisaded mound and ditch, each with its own army and leader, the "Jarl," or Earl. Since the Danes were tireless traders and merchants, carrying their commerce in barges to the wharves of inland towns, they taught the Saxon much in the line of commerce; and when King Alfred's son, Edward the Elder, established a law requiring that all buying and selling must be done in a market town before the reeve, or local administrative officer, he gave an added boost to the concentration of business in the boroughs. As Trevelyan put it, "had it not been for the Scandinavian blood infused into our race by the catastrophes of the Ninth Century, less would have been heard in days to come of British maritime and commercial enterprise." The intrepid Danes, or Norsemen, were found not only in England and in Normandy; they penetrated into Spain, the Mediterranean, and the Levant, and some of these amazing explorers even touched the coast of North America five hundred years before Columbus. But England's indebtedness to those Viking invaders was not only one of racial heritage: it resembled her debt to Rome. For better or for worse, her national development was profoundly affected by belonging to the Scandinavian empire of King Canute and his sons in the eleventh century. That fact prepared the way for the last conquest of the island in 1066.

In 1930 Walter Carruthers Sellars and Robert Julian Yeatman pub-

*A fleet under William the Conqueror crosses the English Channel in 1066 to herald the beginning of Norman rule.*

*Above: King Alfred the Great*
*Right: the Venerable Bede*

lished their memorable history of England, and it went through twenty-eight editions in slightly more than ten years. They called it *1066 and All That,* thereby enshrining the date of the Norman Conquest as the key date of the Englishman's notion not only of his own history but perhaps of all history whatsoever. In fact, of course, nothing either ended or began in 1066. It is best to think of a thin red line drawn across the page at that point. Lord Macaulay once wrote that during the century and a half that followed the Norman Conquest, strictly speaking there is no English history. It was only when he came to the year of the Magna Carta (1215) and the reconciliation of the two peoples, English and Normans, that he thought English history began again. "Here," he wrote, "commences the history of the English nation." There is a good deal to be said for this view, so long as we do not imagine that pre-Conquest history had been, so to say, a waste of time. The fact is that by 1066 the peoples of the oft-conquered island had undergone a thousand years of deeply formative experience. There was nothing decadent about the English who went down before the Normans in 1066. They were still the people who had bred Bede and Alcuin; they were the fair-haired farmers, the brave fighters, Europe's finest artists in metals, a race of soldier-poets, the people who were to produce Chaucer and Shakespeare.

Some characteristics of the English, recurrent in their history, had already shown themselves clearly among the Anglo-Saxons. Whole books of their riddles have survived; and their fondness for such wordplay, for puns, proverbs, and nicknames, is still a noticeable characteristic of their descendants who follow quiz programs on radio and television and labor over crossword puzzles in newspapers and magazines. Most precious of all, as a historic legacy, is the old English attachment to direct speech: the simple and passionate prose of Cobbett and Defoe springs from a peculiarly English manner of expression, which is first evident in the downright pragmatic speech of Bede, as in his immortal allegory of the sparrow flying from the wintry blasts into the warmth of the hall, the image of the soul of man passing from eternity to eternity. Here, it has been said, we recognize a certain English way of looking at things, a noble simplicity and freshness not to be heard again until Chaucer.

CHAPTER II

# ENGLISH BEGINNINGS

The Norman Conquest of England has been called the greatest take-over in the history of western Europe. At the head of the enterprise was William, duke of Normandy, the descendant of a Viking chieftain; the men who came with him were a motley throng of Normans, Flemings, and Bretons. The duke of Normandy was making good his claim that the English Crown had been promised to him by his cousin, the childless King Edward the Confessor (*r.* 1042–66). Whether or not this was so, the Crown, being elective, was not Edward's to give; and at the Confessor's death the English witan, or assembly of notables, had chosen Harold, earl of Wessex, as Edward's successor.

The difficulty was that Harold, when he had been shipwrecked on the coast of Normandy in 1064, had also sworn to acknowledge William's claim. So William may be said to have come to take what was his by two promises. The story was recounted some twenty years later by the ladies who embroidered the Bayeux Tapestry. This famous relic, fashioned in colored wools on a strip of coarse linen 230 feet long and about 20 inches wide, is a priceless if somewhat

*Fortified castles proliferated as a result of the Norman Conquest.*

biased historical record. It is a graphic account of the story of the Conquest and what led up to it, but it depicts these events as the Normans wanted that story to be believed.

After Harold's coronation early in 1066—an event accompanied by the ominous portent of Halley's comet—two separate invasion forces set out almost simultaneously for England. The first was from Scandinavia, led by one of Canute's successors, Harald Haardraade, king of Norway; the other was from Normandy. Harold dealt skillfully with the Norsemen, defeating them at the bloody battle of Stamford Bridge, and almost at the moment of victory news reached him that William had landed at Pevensey. On October 14, after making a forced march and gathering all the reinforcements he could assemble on short notice, Harold and the battered survivors of Stamford Bridge took up a position across William's route to London, on the spur of a hill six miles northwest of Hastings—a site marked today by the village and abbey of Battle. As the Normans approached, the Anglo-Saxons left their horses in the rear, and formed on foot in their customary shield-ring, armed with long Danish battle-axes. The mounted Norman knights, storming the hillside, were supported by volleys of arrows fired between charges by ranks of archers in their rear, and the superiority of arms and tactics finally proved too much for the defenders. When dusk fell, Harold and the men of his bodyguard lay dead at the foot of the royal standard, surrounded by hundreds of slain comrades, while the survivors scattered in all directions before the Norman cavalry. Duke William, who had fought in the front ranks and had three horses killed beneath him, could claim the victory; he could also assert that his claim to the throne of England had been vindicated by the god of battles. The throne was his by both heredity and conquest, which twofold argument put him in a very strong position. What he could not do as lawful heir he could do by the right which springs from might. As hereditary king, he could call out the militia, and he could impose the Danegeld, a tax which the Saxon kings had levied in order to pay off the Danish invaders in the tenth century. As conqueror, William could do almost anything else.

The Norman Conquest, indeed, established a despotic monarchy. Not only this, it established the Norman in place of the English aristocracy. The Conqueror apportioned the land among his followers bit by bit as he conquered it, which necessarily meant that no one acquired too much in any one place—an arrangement that made for the security of the king. Thus was created the aristocracy of medieval England, or the "barons," a class of men upon whom the king depended considerably for the defense and government of his realm. Centuries later, English radicals like Tom Paine were to ask the question, "Who are the aristocracy?" and to answer, "William the Conqueror's colonels, his majors, and his captains." Both question and answer were intended to have pejorative overtones, and yet if the Norman aristocracy had not been military men, and good men of business, the conquered land would have lacked both order and administration. It certainly would never have become, as William intended it should, a going concern.

The Conqueror was the bastard son of Robert, duke of Normandy, and a girl called Harlève whom he had seen dancing in the road, or, it is also told, washing clothes in the stream. Harlève must have been a remarkable woman, for her son was strong, self-willed, and (as men said in those days) "worshipful." His conquest was ruthless, as was shown by the "harrying of the north," which devastated hundreds of miles of northern England with a scorched-earth thoroughness worthy of General Sherman (but without his excuse, for William had already won the war). It was the "harsh beginning of much," to use Thomas Carlyle's phrase, signalling the bloody entry of England into the mainstream of European civilization. The duke continued to rule his dukedom on the other side of the Channel, and the propinquity of his two dominions brought much, both good and ill, to the island. Soon England began to bear the typical marks of a civilization that lived by land, built in stone, and thought in the language of military might. The beauty instituted by this new influence is still visible in the clean-cut masonry of castle and cathedral raised by a military aristocracy and a militant church.

The Conqueror sent out *enquêteurs,* or inquirers, to take an inventory of his new possessions. In compiling that unique record known as the Domesday Book, it was almost as if William had a care for the future writers of history. As the writers of the time tell us in the Anglo-Saxon Chronicle: "So narrowly did he cause the survey to be made that there was not one single hide nor rood of land, nor—it is

OVERLEAF: *a scene from the Bayeux Tapestry shows Norman cavalrymen suffering a temporary setback at the hands of their British adversaries.*

ERA NCI: INPRELIO:

shameful to tell but he thought it no shame to do—was there an ox, cow or swine that was not set down in the writ." The Domesday Book was the only thing of its kind in western Europe, a memorial to a great race of businessmen and an indication that the easy-going ways of the Saxons were at an end. Post-Conquest England kept books and struck balances.

There was to be much dispute among historians over the question of continuity or new beginnings in 1066; over what was changed by the Conquest that was important in English life, and what persisted in spite of the Norman invasion. At the time, most people would have noticed only that one aristocracy had replaced another, and that the Norman possession of the land brought with it a definition of social categories and their relations one to another. Also, the Church became urbanized. The conquerors were scandalized to find the Saxon prelates living like farmers, so—by order of the Conqueror himself—the churchmen now went to live in the towns and ceased to sit on the bench of the shire court. In the future, the Church with its great officers and its own courts was to exist apart from the secular hierarchy.

Now the great Norman towers of cathedrals and parish churches began to show how much the clergy resembled the military aristocracy of the Normans. The very language of government and administration, and soon of literature itself, lost much of its Saxon rudeness and flowed along in the more polite forms of Norman French. Although their commemorative brass effigies on church floors often make them seem strange, even comic, figures, in their time the Normans were, nevertheless, the ablest warriors and governors in Europe. Taking it all in all, and despite its brutalities, the Norman Conquest was a positive achievement. A strong monarchy, a proud aristocracy, a purified church, a vigorous urban life, and a language fit to take its place among the literary tongues of Europe: all these and much more came as a result of the Conquest, launching the country on a Continental course while yet preserving all that was best in the island on the edge of the world. As men were later to say, while England was proud of being an island, she was never to forget that she belonged to Europe.

The economy of England in the Anglo-Norman period was almost

*A rubbing from a tomb effigy commemorates a Norman nobleman.*

 entirely agrarian and, as the Domesday Book reveals, was largely organized on a manorial basis. The land was farmed on a "strip" system by a large variety of dependent classes of cultivators, of whom the great majority were villeins or serfs. These strips of land generally made up three large fields ranging away from the manor house and the parish church, and fringed with wasteland and woodland where the dependent occupiers could pasture their beasts, feed their hogs on acorns or beech mast, and cut turf and fuel. There was a good deal of cooperative plowing, although the villagers held their arable strips in individual occupation. They paid services or dues in money or kind to the lord of the manor, working for so many days a week on his land, and they were bound to attend his court.

After the Conquest there was a wholesale depression of the laboring classes. In fact, all classes of the native population were downgraded by the Conquest, but the lowest class naturally felt the weight of depression most because its members were at the bottom of the heap. They found themselves doing the work of slaves, and thus a nation of free villagers was transformed into a nation of serfs. Generations passed before they recovered the status enjoyed by the Saxon freemen. For a time, and for the mass of Englishmen, although learned men have often tried to minimize it, the Norman Conquest was a tragedy.

The manorial organization of rural society, with its obligations extending both upward and downward between lord and man, has the generic name of the "feudal system," although it only assumed the neat character of a system long after the fact at the hands of lawyers and antiquarians. Actually, feudalism is nothing but a shorthand term for a whole complex of social relationships which prevailed all over Europe for several centuries. The main social bond in a feudal state of society was the relationship of lord and man—the obligation on the lord's part being protection and defense, that of the man being reverence and service in daily labor and in arms. By this system of mutual obligation, resting on a basis of land, the business of society in all its aspects was carried on. In medieval England hardly anyone saw anything oppressive or unjust about this system. Of course, the top men in such a society could, and not infrequently did, act in an arbitrary fashion, but the feudal superior was unlikely to injure, let alone destroy, his dependent men any more than he would do away with his draft animals, and the feudal dependent was unlikely to regard himself as the victim of the system, for the most painful position in medieval society was to be outside it, to be a "landless man." Indeed, the whole system depended for its working on mutual tolerance and obligation. It is from feudal society that is derived the phrase *noblesse oblige,* which simply means "rank imposes obligations."

In the Middle Ages, and for some time afterward, the history of England revolves around the person and the personality of the king. He did not merely reign, he actually governed. The peace and good governance of the realm depended on a stable succession and a line of strong characters. If the monarch failed, or misgoverned, his vassals drew together and filled his place as well as they were able. It is impossible to understand the nature of feudalism unless one grasps the fact that the barons, often considered to have been a chronically disorderly force in medieval English society, were an essential part of the system and not alien or inimical to it. There was no irrepressible conflict between them and the king. "Whatever the system might be, they [the barons] were part of it," one historian has said. "Indeed there is little exaggeration in saying that they *were* it." What, after all, was the king but a superbaron? It is true that once he had been crowned, invested with the mystic potency bestowed on him by the holy oil at his coronation, everyone knew that he was something different, superior to all earthly men, for was he not the Lord's Anointed? He was supposed to be endowed with magical curative powers, and for generations mothers would take their children into the royal presence to be "touched," as Samuel Johnson was taken as a child by his mother to be cured of the scrofula (the "king's evil") by Queen Anne. This magic notion of monarchy survived for hundreds of years in the minds of European peoples.

For long enough the writing of history was dominated by the mystique of monarchy. Indeed, in 1874 John Richard Green felt obliged to write an apologetic introduction to his *Short History of the English People* because he had decided to make it a history of the English *people:* "The aim of the following work," he said, "is defined by its title; it is a history, not of English Kings or English Con-

*A pictorial record of England's Norman kings begins with William at top left.*

quests, but of the English People. . . . I have preferred to pass lightly and briefly over the details of foreign wars and diplomacies, the personal adventures of kings and nobles, the pomp of courts, or the intrigues of favourites. . . . I have devoted more space to Chaucer than to Cressy, to Caxton than to the petty strife of Yorkist and Lancastrian. . . ." 

Whether or not Green's way of writing history needed apology, there is little doubt that to write it in terms of a succession of kings and queens fostered an emphasis on continuity. Anyone who wants to do so can gain an impression of the continuity of English history most readily by tracing it along the line of monarchy. It is something of which the English themselves have always been proud. In Geoffrey of Monmouth's *Historia regum Britanniae,* which was written early in the twelfth century, probably at Oxford, where historical research has always been pieced out with imagination, Geoffrey was not content to trace the monarchy back to King Arthur—he took it down to Brutus the Trojan. A revolution, a deposition, an abdication, is not permitted to break the thread but is industriously woven into the fabric. When cleavage does occur and resists the process, English historians and publicists exercise vast ingenuity in trying to prove that it is illusory, or so inconsequential as not to matter. The English historian Herbert Butterfield has said, ". . . we seek to join up again, as though it mattered to us to maintain the contact with the past." It is almost as if the nation's strength depends upon keeping in touch with a continuous past, as Antaeus had to maintain contact with the firm earth lest he lose his strength.

Thus the most notable break in the history of England, the Norman Conquest, was promptly patched into the pattern of continuity, first by refusing to call it a conquest, and then by calling the conquest a myth. For good tactical reasons, the conquerors themselves assisted in this process by their conduct at the time, covering over as many cracks as they could.

The monarchy went through two phases in the century and a half following the Norman Conquest. The first was the reign of William I himself, and that of two of his sons—William II (*r.* 1087–1100) and Henry I (*r.* 1100–1135)—followed by his grandson, Stephen. These years were occupied by royal endeavors to strengthen their position by bidding for the support of the depressed English against the Norman aristocracy. William I continued the life of the old local courts of shire and hundred, and promised the maintenance of the laws of King Edward. William II sought popularity with the vanquished English by calling them *Anglos suos . . . probos et fortes viros* (His English . . . strong and true). This policy of conciliation came to fruition under Henry I, who, in face of rivals and rebels, pursued a steady policy of drawing the defeated English to his side so that his Norman lords deplored their king's habit of playing up (or down) to the conquered race and even called him "the last king of the English." He married Matilda, the Saxon princess, thus uniting the Norman and Saxon lines and reconciling the two peoples. Since Matilda was directly descended from King Alfred, this marriage makes the present queen of England the lineal descendant of Alfred over a period of precisely eleven hundred years.

Henry I went further, and he offered his subjects more than flattery and promises. Having to compete for the throne with another brother, Robert, he made his biggest bid for popularity by putting forth a Charter of Liberties at his coronation and having copies sent to every shire. In it he promised to maintain the laws of King Edward—the good old English laws. This document was brought out as a model when the barons extorted the Great Charter, the Magna Carta, from King John a century later.

When the first Henry died of overeating, a monk wrote that there was "treason soon in the land, for every man that could forthwith robbed another." In Henry's day, a man could walk about the kingdom with his gold and silver safely in his purse, but none could say as much for the reign of his successor, King Stephen (*r.* 1135–54), which was remembered as the "nineteen long winters," when, men said, "God and his angels slept." Stephen was reported by contemporaries to have been the "mildest of men upon earth, the slowest to take offense, the readiest to pardon . . ."—in fact, the most unsuitable man to be king of an unruly feudal state. A grandson of the Conqueror and a nephew of Henry I, he was opposed in his claim to the throne by Matilda, or Maud, a daughter of Henry and the wife of Geoffrey, count of Anjou. While the two of them quarreled and raised rival armies, the king's authority was steadily diminished as a result of what might be described as unchecked feudalism. As a chronicler wrote, "Every powerful man made his castles and held them against the King . . . and when the castles were made they filled them with devils and evil men." As a consequence, "With some men the love of country was turned to loathing and bitterness, and they preferred to migrate to distant regions. Others . . . passed their lives in fear and anguish." Finally the death of Stephen put an end to this chaotic period, by bringing to the throne a man born to rule.

England's second monarchal phase was that of the Angevin family, the dukes of Anjou, which began with the accession of Matilda's son, Henry Plantagenet, who was crowned Henry II in 1154. He was a man of medium size, thickset and bull-necked, with powerful arms and legs bowed from endless riding, close-cropped hair, a violent temper, and boundless animal energy. Traveling constantly about his dominions with an exhausted retinue behind him, he was England's first truly international figure on the European stage. While in England, he went directly about the business of recovering lands that had been lost to the Crown under Stephen, and in serving his own interests by establishing certain legal procedures, he also served the realm. English law and its modes of procedure were neither invented under, nor by, Henry II; instead, the law became articulate, developing—after some years—into a habit of legal practice, with its writs and its forms of action, its juries and its assizes. It was almost as if the monarchy, having established its strength and authority with the Conqueror and his sons, was now to equip itself with the institutions which, in due course, would amount to a constitution. It has never been possible to read the English constitution in a single document or body of documents which describe a set of institutions and their working. Rather it is a complex of operative instruments evolved out of royal necessities in dealing with day-to-day problems. Councils, law courts, juries, writs, taxes—all were created pragmatically. Setting them to work on the diurnal needs of government, the king made sure that they worked.

Henry II's celebrated quarrel with the Church came about, in considerable part, because of his campaign for the rule of law. He was unlucky enough to have in Thomas à Becket an archbishop of Canterbury who was prepared to outpope the bishop of Rome—Alexander

III—in the cause of what he believed to be justice and righteousness, although one of the more moderate churchmen of the day observed that the dignitaries of the Church "were more intent on defending the liberties and rights of the clergy than on correcting and restraining their vices." Becket had previously been Henry's chancellor, his boon companion, his ally in the early and arduous years of the recovery of the realm from the anarchy of Stephen's reign, and that made the quarrel the more bitter, as did the fact that after becoming archbishop of Canterbury in 1162, Becket showed himself to be an extremist in everything he undertook. The dispute centered on the trial of priests who had committed civil crimes, with the king asserting it as his right to try and to punish a clerk of the Church who had been tried and acquitted in ecclesiastical court. It was a head-on collision, of course, between state and church, and it became a vindictive personal fight as well between the two strong-willed men. At last Becket left the realm to spend six years in self-imposed exile, during which he fulminated against the king from pulpits on the Continent; then he returned to England, and on Christmas Day 1170 he denounced and excommunicated his enemies from the pulpit at Canterbury. A few days later he was murdered in the cathedral. Henry did penance for the foul deed and was absolved, after agreeing to abolish all customs injurious to the Church. So Becket won the battle by his martyrdom, but the war between state and church would continue, unresolved, for four more centuries.

Henry II had to govern a Continental empire that stretched from the Channel to the Pyrenees. He had Normandy from his mother, Anjou from his father, Poitou in right of his wife, and these were only a part of his dominion. He held more of the land of France than the king of France did; England was only a rather disorderly corner of the great complex that called him king. This was good for England, for it took him away from the island a great deal of the time, and the English had to learn to get on without him. It also brought the country experience of French institutions. Many of Henry's procedures which were to become most identified with England were derived from the practices of Frankish kings, one of these probably being the jury. The English acquired not a little of their celebrated gift for self-government from the absenteeism of rulers like Henry II and from the need of a ruler of extensive

*An ivory carving depicting the murder of Thomas à Becket in Canterbury Cathedral by Henry II's henchmen*

European possessions to delegate a fair share of the work, for the king's servants, sheriffs, itinerant judges, and the rest were very busy men under Henry II. The able men he trained in the tasks of government carried the process of delegation even further under his son, Richard I, known as Coeur de Lion, who spent much of his ten-year reign with sword in hand on campaign in the Holy Land.

In 1192 Richard was taken prisoner and required to be ransomed by the payment of 150,000 marks. The task of raising this inordinate sum afforded his subjects the experience of devising an extensive scheme of taxation, and in 1195 another problem posed by the king's absence was solved by an edict requiring everyone over fifteen years of age to take an oath to keep the peace and assist in the capture of malefactors. Certain knights who were appointed to receive these oaths were probably the germ of what later ages would know as justices of the peace. The fiscal and judicial tasks imposed by measures like these caused William Stubbs, the great Victorian scholar, to call the reign of Richard I an age of "self-agency," when the people became used to self-government.

"Lo!" men said when they contemplated the functions of monarchy in medieval times, "to fight and to judge is the office of a King!" The Angevins did both with zest, nor did they specialize overmuch. While Henry II is best remembered for his law reforms and juries and assizes for the administration of justice, he spent much of his time at war for the maintenance of his empire. Richard I was the epitome of the medieval warrior-king, on crusade for the recovery of the Holy Sepulchre from the infidel Turks and their great leader Saladin. He managed to take Jaffa, but was brought to make a truce with Saladin on the way to Jerusalem. He met his death, however, warring against one of his French vassals.

The culmination of the Angevin age, following the age of the Norman Conquest, came with the reign of King John, who succeeded his brother Richard in 1199. John was the youngest son of Henry II, and like the other sons of that remarkable ruler he was highly intelligent, almost frenetically active, and often intolerably willful. He ended by offending every section of his people. Like Richard, he was an excellent soldier, but he was never so happy as when personally presiding in his courts of law. By 1204 he had lost his French lands north of the Loire to the king of France, which outraged his feudal vassals who held land

*Richard I witnessing the execution of 2,600 Saracen prisoners at Acre*

there. This was what provoked their rising against him and the exaction of the Magna Carta, or Great Charter of 1215.

The other element in the opposition was his quarrel with the Church over the election of Stephen Langton as archbishop of Canterbury. His father's dispute with Thomas Becket had been part of his great campaign to assert the law of the land over all his subjects, clergy as well as laity. John's feud with Langton, however, led to the pope's placing England under interdict, which amounted to a general strike on the part of the clergy. The king retaliated by confiscating the property of the clergy, a move that brought excommunication upon him. Not only were his people deprived of all religious rites, but the king was declared deposed, and the pope ordered John's old enemy, the king of France, to execute the order of deposition. Cut off from the body of Christendom and an outcast among his own people, King John could only submit, receive Stephen Langton as archbishop, and agree to hold England as a papal fief, paying an annual tribute of one thousand marks. Langton then produced Henry I's Charter of Liberties before the assembled barons, and after the king had been defeated along with his Continental allies by the king of France at the battle of Bouvines, he was compelled to set his seal to the Magna Carta at Runnymede in June, 1215. He died next year in the midst of a French invasion. Less than seventy years separated his wretched death at Newark from the triumph of his father, the first of his line. When John died, leaving a child of nine at the head of his distraught kingdom, the barons and prelates at once assumed responsibility for the "state" of the Crown until the king should come of age. It was not to their advantage that the kingdom should lapse into disorder. Here is a clear instance of the vital role the barons played in the feudal system.

In all of this, the nation was the victor. The loss of Normandy to the French was something that would have come about inevitably, in time, and it rid England of an expensive, dangerous appendage which could only prove another source of friction between the Channel neighbors. Without this distraction, England could turn energy and thought to her own affairs. But John's barons did not see it that way; failing to perceive that the Angevin empire had had no intrinsic unity, they viewed the loss as a humiliating defeat, and took out their anger on a monarch already suspect in the eyes of the nobility. The winning of the Charter may be said to mark another vital turning point. Lord Macaulay claimed that for the century and a half of Norman tyranny there had been, strictly speaking, no English history. The Magna Carta, he held, was the upsurge of the unconquerable English love of liberty, and this despite the fact that it was wrung from the king by the feudal baronage and was in its principal contents a charter of feudal privileges registering the special rights—or privileges—of special classes of people, mostly barons and bishops. Such liberties as were vindicated in medieval times were not so much the achievement of an inherently liberty-loving people as reluctant concessions extracted from an embarrassed monarchy.

For centuries the English were to look back to the Great Charter for the credentials of such cherished principles as "no taxation without representation" and "no imprisonment without trial." Every word of this famous document has been said to be worth a king's ransom. It is not perpetually enshrined beneath special lighting like the American Constitution or the embalmed body of Lenin in the Kremlin, but it is the English counterpart of these things, the palladium of their liberties. When Bishop Stubbs said "the whole of the constitutional history of England is a commentary on this Charter," he scarcely exaggerated more than did Alfred North Whitehead when he said that the whole history of political thought is a series of footnotes to Plato's *Republic*. Besides its obvious benefits to the mighty barons, the Great Charter contained clauses affecting the well-being of merchants, freeholders, and even villeins. But most valuable of all, from the standpoint of later generations, was the total impression to be gained from the mere fact that a king had been compelled to acknowledge certain principles as law which he must observe. There was, in addition, the machinery that could bring him to book if he ignored those principles in the future. Precisely what laws the king was subordinate to would be less important than that he was now proclaimed to be under law.

CHAPTER III

# ENGLAND IN THE LATER MIDDLE AGES

The establishment of the machinery of the English Common Law under the Angevin kings, notably Henry II, and the promulgation of the Magna Carta by King John put England on the road that led to a modern nation-state. The Middle Ages formed one long training period in the sense of order: as the Normans had established the all-governing monarchy, the Angevins founded the rule of law. It was within these conditions that order could subsist and flourish. During these medieval centuries England was apprenticed to the habits of systematic life and thinking which in turn made possible the scientific achievements of the modern world—achievements which depend, as the philosopher Alfred North Whitehead put it, upon "the inexpungable belief that every detailed occurrence can be correlated with its antecedents in a perfectly definite manner, exemplifying general principles."

This training, or experience, was acquired by men in the activities of common life as it was lived in the cloister, in the law courts, in the workshop—places where men sought to save their souls, defend their practical interests, and produce the means to life. The by-product of

*Salisbury Cathedral, with its lofty spires, looms above the landscape.*

their activities in these pursuits, a primitive rationalism, was what we call the "scientific attitude." Indeed, faith in the *possibility* of science was generated antecedently to the development of modern science. It came out of the business of government. Little by little the king contrived to harness his household officers to the administration of his kingdom, found new ways of tapping the wealth of woolmen and clothiers in the form of taxes, brought knights and burgesses to his council to strike bargains with them—bargains that brought him wealth and them privileges. Similarly, when a royal writ set in motion a certain legal process to determine the rightful possessor of a particular piece of land, it took men's minds through an intellectual process, an exercise in logic, the evaluation of evidence, the rationale of cause and effect, the discovery of the processes of organized life, transcending mere chance or arbitrary mystery by experience of the order of nature. A disputation in a cloister, a cathedral school, a university, did the same thing, so that there is after all nothing absurd in calling the possibility of modern science an "unconscious derivative of medieval theology." When men conducted experiments in stresses and strains to hold up a wall containing more glass than stone, they were discovering the elements of basic engineering. Common-lawyers, canonists, schoolmen, masons, all were working in their several fields in ways that made possible the modern world as we know it.

In England this process went along lines laid down under the Norman and Angevin kings. Reign by reign, generation by generation, kings and barons quarreled and fought and came to terms in the daily business of government. Century by century, a technical revolution in architecture transformed the face of the land with ramparts of stone and soaring walls of glass, while all the time the plow, unaltered, traced the ancient pattern of agriculture. Transformation and change proceeded at an entirely different pace in the cathedral than in the cornfield, for development was dependent on the wealth and intelligence of an aristocracy in church and state. Culture, civilization, technical improvement, may come of a need for more food in a hungry world; a medieval cathedral came of no such necessity, but of the pomp and pride and piety of great churchmen and their patrons. The marvels of medieval art were created amidst the squalor of a world where the toil of common men had made the land rich enough to be able to afford it.

The thirteenth and the fourteenth centuries were the high-water mark of English civilization in the Middle Ages. They saw the glories of stained glass and the pointed arch, the birth of the first great poetry, and a truly significant political development: long before 1400 the king was already expanding his council to include representatives of shires and boroughs in what would soon become the House of Commons. As parliament (from the word meaning "parley" or "discussion") was an invention of the Middle Ages, so was the university. For centuries, what higher learning there was had been the domain of the Church; then, in the twelfth and thirteenth centuries, universities suddenly sprang up in Europe and, with the founding of Oxford and Cambridge, in England. Men of privilege—the barons and knights—regarded a university education as beneath them, and the villein could not aspire to one, so the students were usually sons of yeomen and retainers, for whom an education might prove a leg up to a higher place. At this time, the typical student was likely to be a bright lad, of very modest means, from a lower middle-class background, who came up to Oxford or Cambridge at the age of fourteen and stayed for seven or eight years, engaged chiefly in the study of logic.

All these great developments took place amidst the turbulence and tragedy of the twin medieval horrors, war and plague. No one can compute the extent of mortality in the Hundred Years' War, but it is reasonably estimated that the terrible pestilence from Asia known as the Black Death had swept away nearly half the population of England by the end of the fourteenth century, and that the number of inhabitants of the island remained almost stationary for many years. It was one of the most appalling catastrophes in the history of mankind. In Europe the Black Death broke out first in Constantinople in 1333 and, spreading rapidly from one unsanitary town to another, crossed the Continent, killing anywhere from one fourth to three fourths of the population. Reaching England, it reduced the number of Edward III's subjects from four million to something like two and a half million within the span of sixteen months. The character of the disease itself was hideous enough; the effects of the pestilence on English society were almost beyond comprehension. We read of villages that ceased to exist, of monasteries where half the inmates perished, of parish churches whose vicars, performing the last offices, could scarcely keep ahead of the deaths. In

East Anglia alone, eight hundred priests died. For most people life was, as the philosopher Thomas Hobbes said of man's lot in the state of nature, "solitary, poor, nasty, brutish and short," and the art of the later Middle Ages recorded grimly the waiting terrors of mortality, depicting in wall paintings and poetry the charnel house, skulls grinning over graves, masques enacting the dance of death. The concept of Merrie England was an invention of a later age, when men looked back from the smoke of "dark, satanic mills," and thought to discern medieval peasants drinking ale and dancing round maypoles. Out of sorrow and suffering, blood, toil, tears, and sweat, came forth the world we know, for good and ill.

Following the momentous misrule of King John there came the ineffectual government of Henry III, the saintly man who built Westminster Abbey, the national shrine of later ages. Under him there had to be certain attempts at government by baronial councils, and his reign ended with the assembly of the first truly representative parliament, albeit packed by Simon de Montfort with his supporters. Montfort, the French-born earl of Leicester who married Henry's sister, had become a sworn enemy of the king and led the barons in a war against him. He emerged as the most important figure in the realm until Edward Plantagenet, the Prince of Wales, led the royal troops to a victory over the barons, in the course of which Montfort was killed. When Henry III died in 1272, the Prince of Wales was away on crusade, but he was proclaimed king as Edward I, and government carried on in his name. It is at this point that the celebrated dictum, "Le roi est mort, vive le roi!" had its inception.

Edward was the true giant of the time. He was a man of huge energy and intelligence as well as of imposing physical stature: according to the chronicler Nicholas Trivet, he stood a head and shoulders above the ordinary man. He had thick hair, which changed from yellow in childhood to black, and finally to white; and his regular features were marred only by the drooping lid of his left eye. For his long legs he was nicknamed Longshanks, and he delighted in tournaments, war, and that substitute for war—hunting. In mental and moral stature he was remarkable, too, his only grave defect being a readiness to assume that anyone who opposed him must be wicked. This characteristic, along with a certain legalistic shiftiness, may account for his failure to cap-

*One hundred Oxford dons meet with their warden at New College in 1461.*

ture the unalloyed enthusiasm of posterity despite his great qualities as a ruler and a soldier. By blood a product of southern Europe (he was son, grandson, and great-grandson of women of Provence and Aquitaine), he was to rule over the vast Continental estates he had inherited, as well as over England. He was in some respects the first truly English monarch—a man under whom the union of Norman and Saxon at last became reality; and such were his territorial interests that he could, and did, identify himself with Christendom as a whole. It seems that all his great undertakings, which included the subjugation of Wales, not to mention his attempt to codify English law in a succession of great statutes (which led to his being called the English Justinian), were intended as preparatory to his leadership of a great crusade for the relief of Jerusalem. As he drew near to the completion of these tasks, he died on a campaign to subdue the Scots.

Edward I's concern with the rescue of the Holy Land is typical of his slightly old-fashioned ambitions. His lot was cast in a wonderful time, the High Middle Ages—the age of Giotto, Dante, and Roger Bacon, of the great glories of Gothic art. How far he was aware of all this we do not know, for we have little record of either intellectual or artistic interests on his part. After all, he was dominated always and everywhere by the exigencies of war and law and politics, laying the foundations of an empire that was to be known one day as Great Britain. It is only in the field of war and politics that we see him at work and can dimly trace the interplay of old and new ideas. His attitude toward feudalism is revealed by his great statutes, many of which seem to ignore the fact that the traditional relations of lord and vassal were already fading into those of sovereign and subject after the style of the modern world, although it is difficult to believe that he did not quite know what he was doing or what was happening. For the future benefit of England, however, he had both the political insight and a long enough reign to identify the state of the king with the well-being of the community. It is in that sense alone, and not because he had any deep-laid plans for the future of parliamentary government, that Edward I is remembered still as the father of parliamentary representation. His contribution to the success of parliamentary institutions was purely incidental to the tasks of government. The common task and practical experience taught him that the king's weight and influence in affairs would be increased

*Edward II represented on a tomb sculpture*

rather than diminished by his cooperation not only with his barons but with the commonalty at large: in other words that *commune concilium regni* was likely to be most serviceable if it was really common.

England had great men and great rulers in plenty. Perhaps Edward was the kingdom's finest, both in his general humanity and in the vastness of his undertakings. His name is usually placed second only to that of King Alfred. The reigns of those towering medieval kings are like the waves of an incoming tide: after each there is a trough, generally a recession. Upon the death of Edward I, his son became king as Edward II. This new ruler was hardly a worthy successor to his father, being much influenced by a foolish favorite called Piers Gaveston, and preferring occupations like thatching and smithying to governance. He was deposed and horribly put to death in 1327 to make way for another man of more kingly stature, his son, and the grandson of King John, Edward III.

The most important influences on English life and fortunes in the fourteenth century, however, were not men or institutions but events: the outbreak of the Hundred Years' War with France in 1337, and the outbreak of the Black Death some ten years later. We should speak of the *first* Hundred Years' War, for there were to be two more century-long contests between the old enemies: one instigated by the ambitions of Louis XIV in the seventeenth century, and the other set off by Anglo-French colonial ambitions and merging into the wars of the French Revolution and of Napoleon. The first, which may be said to have begun when King John lost the Continental possessions of both Crown and baronage in 1204, was in origin a family quarrel, or a dynastic struggle. It was carried on most successfully by Edward III, who is sometimes known as the patron saint of chivalry. Edward's queen, Philippa of Hainault, had for a time as her secretary Jean Froissart, the author of the classic chronicle that celebrated the cult of chivalry, and Edward established the most ancient and noble Order of the Garter, England's highest order of knighthood. Inspired by the legend of the Arthurian Round Table, the order was formally inaugurated in 1348, membership being limited to the sovereign and twenty-five other knights, including Edward III's eldest son, the Black Prince. By tradition the order's emblem, the blue garter, dates to an incident at a ball in Calais, when Joan, the Fair Maid of Kent (who later married the

*French forces being repulsed by English longbowmen at Crécy*

 Black Prince) lost her garter while dancing, and the king returned it to her with the words, "Honi soit qui mal y pense."

Edward made a cult of war, managing to combine chivalric trappings with a keen regard for its material dividends. Chivalry was entirely an aristocratic concept, and has undergone enormous satire at the hands of Mark Twain and William Makepeace Thackeray in a later age. There is no doubt that what is called chivalry has added greatly to the charm of medieval English history, but in fiction it has involved much anachronistic nonsense. Its best feature, and most influential for the future, was its inculcation of respect for, not to say worship of, women. The word *chivalry* is derived from the Latin *caballus,* meaning horse, since the knight was, of course, a mounted warrior. When war began to be an increasingly serious business, kings relied more and more on mercenaries to do their fighting and on the new merchant class for financial support, thus greatly diminishing the importance of the nobility. Fearing for their prestige and privileges, the knights leaned heavily on the chivalric code as a means of preserving their social status against encroachment.

There were, essentially, three separate forms of chivalry: the oldest was the feudal variety, which stressed above all the virtues and duties of the warrior; there was religious chivalry, which emphasized the knight's obligations to the Church and to his fellow man; and romantic or courtly chivalry, whose ideals were the genteel aspects of knightly conduct, and which was promulgated particularly by the ladies of France and by their itinerant propagandists—the minstrels. Under the code, a knight owed fealty to God, his spiritual master; to the king, his temporal master; and to his sworn love, the mistress of his heart. Among the trouvères, or court poets, of northern France, there was a tendency to favor the mutuality of courtly love over the platonic ideal, and to this tradition the stories of the adulterous relationship of Lancelot and Guinevere trace their origin. The chivalric code was and could be a powerful force, as for example, during the Hundred Years' War, when King John of France returned himself voluntarily to captivity when the ransom demanded by his captor could not be raised; or when, after crushing the French at Poitiers, the Black Prince treated his defeated enemy with the ceremony due his rank, seating him in his own chair, and serving him food with his own hands. (The code was not always observed, however; certainly it did nothing to mitigate the appalling brutalities of war as conducted by the Black Prince in southern France, where he and his marauding knights behaved like freebooters.)

The Hundred Years' War was ostensibly fought over Edward III's claim to the Crown of France, but it was really more to do with safeguarding the wool trade between England and Flanders—the staple of England's exports, and a source of great wealth—which was threatened by French aggression. During its long course, four generations of Englishmen embarked upon plundering expeditions to France as part of a phenomenon noted by the chronicler Froissart. "The English," he observed, "will never love or honour their king, unless he be victorious and a lover of arms and war against their neighbours and especially against such as are greater and richer than themselves. Their land is more fulfilled of riches and all manner of goods when they are at war than in times of peace. They take delight and solace in battles and slaughter: covetous and envious are they above measure of other men's wealth."

The first great defeat of France's feudal armies was a battle that also marked a notable change in military tactics. In the English countryside the longbow had become the yeoman's weapon, and practice with it was one of the principal diversions of village life. At Crécy, in 1346, dismounted English knights fought side by side with massed archers, whose rapid, long-range barrages of cloth-yard shafts destroyed the flower of the French nobility before they could close with Edward III's infantry. As the war went on, the French resorted to thicker armor and substituted plate for chain mail—but the change only cost them mobility and hastened the decline of knighthood and chivalry.

For England's kings, the cost of the war meant greater dependence upon their parliaments, and this at a time when the country was suffering severely from the shortage of labor that followed the Black Death. In the plague's wake, great areas of the countryside had passed out of cultivation; survivors of the pestilence plowed only the most fertile meadows and grazed their herds and flocks on the best pastures. Because of the shortage of plowmen, landlords enclosed their fields and turned the sheep onto them. This coincided with Edward III's importation of skilled Flemish weavers to teach Englishmen the craft, and the beginnings of cloth manufacture in England—developments that offered, for the first time, alternative occupations to the former villeins. Also for the first time is to be seen the spectacle of two masters vying for the services of one man, which produced a general rise of wages, which in turn brought forth the first general Statute of Laborers in an attempt to check it by limiting both wages and prices. As Hegel said, we only learn from history that men never learn anything from history, and thirty years after the Statute of Laborers, as an effect of the attempt to put the clock back, there occurred the widespread social upheaval known as the Peasants' Revolt, a rising of the villeins against serfdom. By that time Edward III was dead and the reigning monarch was that poor unhappy gentleman Richard II, who, after an abortive attempt at despotic rule, abdicated in favor of the first of the line of Lancastrian kings.

Richard II was the cultivated but temperamental man who, as a boy, rode out to meet the peasants in revolt under one Wat Tyler. He pulled the peasant leader from his horse and called upon his followers to take him, King Richard, as their captain. His courage and presence of mind, especially when one of his own followers had stabbed Wat Tyler to the heart, led to the fading out of the revolt in the capital. There could hardly have been a more forthright inauguration of his personal rule.

Unfortunately that rule became too personal, the king letting fall such foolish assertions as that all the laws of England were locked up in his own bosom. High words are of less importance than rash actions in a society where the personal authority of kings prevails, but Richard quarreled persistently with the most powerful and malevolent man of the realm, Henry Bolingbroke, duke of Lancaster. Perhaps in the sea of troubles which was the fourteenth century, an age of feudalism in decline, overmighty subjects, peasant risings, plague, Wyclif and Lollardry (precursors of the Protestant Reformation), Richard believed that he might "by opposing end them"—in other words, that safety lay only in extreme courses. There is not a little of Hamlet's "sweet prince" in Richard, and had he been a man of less gentle character and less imagination, he might yet have outwitted his enemies and kept his crown. As it was, Henry of Lancaster, whom he had banished, returned to claim his inheritance while the king was on campaign in Ireland. In those days it was more than any king's life was worth to turn his back on his enemies even temporarily, and when Richard came home he was forced to abdicate. He died, or was murdered, in jail. Few things are more poignant than Richard's plaint in William Shakespeare's play:

*For God's sake, let us sit upon the ground*
*And tell sad stories of the death of kings . . .*

His departure from the scene in 1399 might be said to mark the close of the English Middle Ages. A king had been deposed and put to death, as Edward II had been in 1327. They talked much in those days of the "divinity that doth hedge a king," and how it kept treason at bay:

*Not all the water in the rough rude sea*
*Can wash the balm from an anointed king . . .*

is what Shakespeare was to make Richard II say. By 1399, however, it looked as if kingship was a hazardous profession in England. (Certainly king killing was no novel practice by the time his subjects cut off the head of Charles I in 1649. It was only the establishment of "king worship" by the intervening Tudors, from Henry VIII to Elizabeth I, that was to invest Charles I with the sobriquet of the Royal Martyr, although his enemies went on calling him the Man of Blood.)

With the passing of Richard II, the "glad confident morning" of medieval England was over, if it had ever existed, and the house of Lancaster, which came to the throne in the person of Henry IV in 1399, gives the impression, rather more than most dynasties, of having been conceived in iniquity and born in sin. Richard's successor lived and died looking over his shoulder, keeping his eye on the shadows which haunt the dark corners of palaces. He was to die confessing that God alone knew by what title he reigned. "Uneasy lies the head that wears a crown," Shakespeare makes him say, and he must have felt especially uneasy when on his deathbed he caught a glimpse of his son trying on the royal crown for size. He suffered from the foreboding conscience that afflicts the usurper, not to speak of the political liabilities of a ruler who knows he must appease the ambitions of the men to whom he owes a large part of his success. The reign of Henry IV used to be termed a period of "premature constitutional government," or of "the Lancastrian Experiment," in which the House of Commons was imagined to have taken more than its customary share in government. It is more likely, however, that under Henry IV parliamentary institutions were

OVERLEAF: *Richard II relinquishing his crown to the duke of Lancaster*

pawns in the power game of noble families. When the Lancastrian Experiment failed for "lack of governance," the house of Tudor was to forget all about the supposed powers and privileges of parliament and to govern England by a popular despotism. For the English, like some other peoples, are readily susceptible to the arguments of Dostoevsky's Grand Inquisitor: that the greatest burden imposed on humanity is the burden of liberty and self-government.

No such doubts and self-questioning afflicted Henry IV's son and heir, generally remembered as Shakespeare's Prince Hal, the fellow reveler of Sir John Falstaff at the Boar's Head tavern. Henry V's historical fortunes were made forever by Shakespeare in glorious verse: his portrait of "Harry the King," the golden-haired athlete who bore the banner of Saint George against such odds in the fields of Flanders, made splendid propaganda for heroic kingship in the later Tudor century, and it is not difficult to imagine that a similar image of this handsome, swashbuckling figure loomed large in the mind of young Henry VIII.

Henry V was engaged in the latest and most glorious phase of the Hundred Years' War begun by his grandfather, Edward III. His army for the invasion of France was an English army raised not by feudal levy but by indentured captains, with six thousand archers paid at sixpence a day, and the king who rode at their head was a seasoned campaigner with the good company commander's understanding of morale and eye for terrain. Invading France in 1415, he took Harfleur by siege and won a dramatic victory at Agincourt against a greatly superior French force. When, two years later, he overran the Île-de-France itself and by the Treaty of Troyes secured his succession to the Crown of France, Henry V commanded a realm extending from the Tweed to the Pyrenees. He had been just in time for glory, for the French were on the eve of their own glorious revival under Joan of Arc, which was to drive the "Goddams," as the English were called, back to their own land. Under Henry V and under the Maid, the old enemies were setting out into the first age of nationalism. By 1453 only Calais remained in the hands of the Goddams.

No doubt when in his play *Saint Joan* Bernard Shaw put the word *nationalism* into the mouth of a political bishop, and the word *Protestantism* into the mouth of the earl of Warwick, and made both of them sense in such modern abstractions the forthcoming doom of feudalism

*After trial by jury in a secular court, a prisoner awaits sentencing.*

*Drawings depicting Henry V during (right) and victorious after (above) the siege of Rouen in 1418*

and the unity of Christendom, he was indulging in somewhat glib anachronism in order to impart a history lesson on the stage, but he was in the largest sense right. As an English nobleman complains, Burgundians and Bretons and Picards and Gascons were beginning to call themselves Frenchmen, and "our fellows are beginning to call themselves Englishmen. . . . They actually talk of France and England as their countries. Theirs, if you please. What is to become of me and you if that way of thinking comes into fashion?" In the earl of Warwick's words, it was all "a cunning device to supersede the aristocracy. . . ." Aristocrats are generally given to thinking that new ideas are specially designed to make the world unsafe for aristocrats. And in the present case they were right. The nation-state, born out of the Hundred Years' War and the Protestant Reformation, among other circumstances, was to prove the deadly enemy of all aristocracies, all hierarchies, whatever. But that development came years later.

Henry V's short-lived victories in France remain one of the highspots in the military experience of a people who have never been militaristic. Time after time their leaders have brought to life memories of such glory in times of national crisis to warm the blood and spur them to victory again, as Harry the King inspired his men before Harfleur by reminding them of the right to victory of men whose fathers "like so many Alexanders, have in these parts from morn till even fought, and sheath'd their swords for lack of argument." It is thus that history makes history. When the old enemy France went down before Hitler's hordes in 1940, Winston Churchill conjured up the vision of Henry V by proposing a joint nationality, an Anglo-French condominium. It came to nothing, but Churchill's words and his actions spoke out of historic memory, even if to the French it was the memory of old, unhappy, far-off things that stood in the way of acceptance of the proposal. As Tocqueville said, one may perish in history from too much memory.

The English are not alone in regarding the hundred years following the deposition of Richard II in 1399 as "futile, bloody and immoral." All over Europe, the sunset of the Middle Ages resembled a blood bath. The amount of blood that was shed in that century of English history —blood of princes, dukes, earls, knights, and simple gentlemen, not to mention plebeian blood of pikemen and men of the longbow—seems

OVERLEAF: *illustrations from Chaucer's* Canterbury Tales

*Squire*

*Miller*

*Reeve*

*Nun's Priest*

*Merchant*

*Monk*

*Clerk of Oxenford*

*Parson*

sufficient in retrospect to float a fleet of battleships. Intermittently during the latter part of the fifteenth century the noble house of York and the noble house of Lancaster bitterly contended for the throne of England. "The Wars of the Roses" is a pretty title for that struggle, which it seems the historian owes to Sir Walter Scott who employed it in a novel in 1829; no one who fought in them thought of them under such a label. The rival families of York and Lancaster, the English were taught at school, plucked white and red roses respectively to deck their hats as they pursued their bloody feud in "fighting for the Crown." The contest was less a quarrel between rival families than it was a family fight, for the contestants were all descendants of the children of Edward III—especially those of John of Gaunt, duke of Lancaster, who begot offspring upon three consorts. The Lancastrians came from the first of his wives, Blanche of Lancaster; the Yorkists descended from Gaunt's brother Lionel, duke of Clarence, after the extinction of the line of the eldest brother, the Black Prince, in the person of his son Richard II. Like most family quarrels, this was long and bitter, and the wars were a series of battles interspersed with periods of armed hostility. Curiously, the countryside as a whole suffered remarkably little, and for the most part, peasants and middle class stood aside, insofar as they were able to do so, and left the fighting to the barons.

To call these wars merely "the fights of kites and crows," as some historians have done, is to be sadly mistaken, for the contestants were fighting over the most fundamental issue in politics in their own, or in any other age: who should wear the crown, the symbol of effective political power? It is the same issue which divides the rival candidates in a parliamentary or a presidential election, only in those days the issue was fought with swords instead of with ballots. And while the fight was on—for some thirty years in the case of the Wars of the Roses—life went on, as life has the splendid habit of doing, very much as usual for the generality of men and women. Foreign visitors, having heard of the constant contentiousness of the English, expressed appreciation of the richness and fertility of the land and its people and the rarity of the expected signs of a war-ravaged country. Above all, it should be remembered that these were the generations when England reaped great profit from the wool trade, as testified by the handsome "wool-churches" that were built in districts—notably East Anglia and the Cotswolds—where social life was dominated by the rich wool merchants. The export of only 5,000 sacks of raw wool (as in the central years of the century, and in the middle of the civil wars) was accounted a recession. When the house of York was winning in the later 1460s, the yearly average export went up to 7,000 and even 9,000. Not for nothing did the piers of Old London Bridge rest upon sacks stuffed with wool, or (as to this day) did the lord chancellor have his seat on the woolsack in the House of Lords.

The century of the contest between Lancaster and York is more recognizable to men and women of the twentieth century than any other of the Middle Ages, for it was an age of violence, of extravagance in dress, and of superstitions. Not only did men kill each other in cold blood after a pitched battle, but they fastened their pointed shoes to their garters, and young men of family liked to be mistaken for "knaves," by wearing their hair long and ragged, their jerkins and nether garments skintight.

Surviving letters between members of the Paston family, who lived in Norfolk in the fifteenth century, bring these people near to us. Here we see parents and children estranged by the "generation gap" of that day, as Margaret Paston writes to her son's tutor, begging that he will "truly belash him" for, she adds, "so did his last master . . . the best he ever had at Cambridge." As for John Paston, sitting at home in their house by the sea, idle, procrastinating, too inert to do anything about his father's grave which still lacked a tombstone, or about his father's house which was drafty and chill with discomfort, John was one of those ambiguous characters who lived on the boundary line where one age merges into another and who do not truly belong to either. His was the world of medieval decadence, yet full of life, and laughing with mischief, as Geoffrey Chaucer portrayed it in poetry that served his age as the novel serves our own. His was an England of springing green, of songbirds, of men and women in whose veins the blood seems to run hot like sap because they live in the beginning of a new world—their world and ours.

CHAPTER IV

# THE DAWN OF EMPIRE

Henry V, the hero of the great English victory over the French at Agincourt, married Catherine of Valois, daughter of Charles VI, the mad king of France, and their eldest child became the fitfully sane Henry VI. When Henry V died Catherine took for her second husband a Welsh gentleman named Owen Tudor, and from this union sprang a new dynasty, one which the English people have always looked upon as peculiarly their own. This remarkable succession of rulers seems to answer to the narcissistic instincts of the nation: in the Tudors the English profess to see those features of which they are most proud, presumably because they believe them to be somehow English, despite the fact that the Tudors were mostly Welsh.

First and foremost among these features is a flair for practical politics, which that family possessed in large measure. Even little Edward VI, who died at fifteen, son of Henry VIII and Jane Seymour, was unmistakably of the breed. His sister, Queen Mary (Bloody Mary), had everything except the capacity to subject her conscience to her political interests, a gift which no other Tudor ever lacked. As for her sister, Elizabeth, the Virgin Queen, she was the greatest political genius who

*Little Moreton Hall, a half-timbered Elizabethan manor house*

 ever wore the crown, and her father, the eighth Henry, had every gift save continence. The first Tudor monarch—Henry VII—set the pattern for his successors, even if he seems in many respects a caricature of them all, more especially in his financial meanness. He was shrewd and penurious, auditing his own accounts, taking care of foreign trade, befriending England's men of business, making his treasury a household office—the king's own chamber—where he made the most of the extensive resources of royal income, investing it, like a financier, in plate and jewelry—the "hard cash" of that day. We forgive Henry VII much, however, when we look upon his sad and beautiful face as portrayed by Pietro Torrigiano. Some of the Tudors were fine scholars, all were personally brave, none—save Mary—ever lacked grasp upon the politically possible. There was not an idealist among them, again with the exception of Mary, and they all died in their beds (except Elizabeth who insisted on dying on the floor propped up on cushions).

Their passion for life was best exemplified by the tall, red-haired, stubborn Henry VIII, possessor of a massive frame, great physical strength, and a huge appetite for food, drink, gambling, and women. A French ambassador who resided for some months at his court admitted later that he never approached the king without fear of physical violence. Another diplomat left a less fearsome portrait: Henry was, he said, "the handsomest potentate I have ever set eyes on; above the usual height, with an extremely fine calf to his leg; his complexion fair and bright, with auburn hair combed straight and short in the French fashion, and a round face so very beautiful that it would become a pretty woman. . . . He speaks French, English, Latin, and a little Italian, plays well on the lute and harpsichord, sings from a book at sight, draws the bow with greater strength than any man in England, and jousts marvellously."

When Machiavelli wrote his manual for crowned, and republican, crooks in power (a manual which they had not read and had no need to read), he declared, "It is unnecessary for a prince to have all the good qualities I have enumerated." But, he continued, "It is very necessary for [him] to appear to have them." If there was to be ill-feeling or unpopularity, the important thing was to see to it that the consequences fell upon other people, preferably ministers, a precept unerringly followed by the Tudors, and fatally followed by the Stuarts. The English who imagine that the Tudors were sensible middle-class rulers, conveniently forget their treachery and their abominable cruelty, especially to rebels. They forget, too, their most intense regality.

They presided over a nation that, like themselves, had its way to make in a dangerous world. At the opening of their rule, their country was small, poor (particularly the monarch), and internationally of little account. France, the ancient enemy, had emerged from the Hundred Years' War greatly strengthened, and the French monarchs now ruled over a nation-state—a united country that reached from the Channel to the Mediterranean. England was a satellite of Spain, the mightiest power in the world. Yet in little more than eighty years England had broken with the mightiest Catholic power and done to death Mary Queen of Scots, pawn of the Counter Reformation, and was going it alone. She did this mainly as a result of the Tudors having launched her upon an age of king worship, and the measure of their success is the length of time it took to bring the people to levy war on the king in the following century. It has been rightly said that hardly anyone wanted to solve problems by having recourse to the sword, so well had the Tudors trained England to prefer law to war. In fact, of course, the Tudors were lawless enough when their own interests were threatened, but they managed to associate their people with them in their ill-doing. After the chronic disorder of the fifteenth century the people preferred to have the king too strong rather than insufficiently strong to put down his, and generally their own, enemies. The "over-mighty subject" was the principal menace to both, though there were many fewer aristocratic or noble traitors than at any other time. There was plenty of treason, but it was always unsuccessful. For one thing the monarchy made it too expensive by imposing heavy fines instead of chopping off traitors' heads, so that it might be said that attempts at treason were made profitable financially to the king. The monarchy also maintained what men called "the high and mighty court of Star Chamber" which could levy these fines on the most powerful people without fear or favor. The Tudors employed also the court of requests which administered even-handed justice between rich and poor, strong and weak—the only "prerogative court" never formally abolished under the Stuarts.

Described thus, Tudor England begins to look in retrospect like an ideal commonwealth, and men who were bred under these skillful

sovereigns were to look back with longing and regret for the passing of the dynasty. They had had little to fear of royal encroachment "in this happy time of lenity . . . under so gracious a prince," as one member of parliament declared under Elizabeth, "yet the times might be altered. . . ." They were indeed. There are few occasions in any people's history when royal despotism—for that indeed is what Tudor rule was—works well enough to be regretted when it gives way to something else. In the next century, men were to fight each other, to cut off the king's head, to abolish the Church and the House of Lords, but these events were to leave no permanent scars on the body politic and, ever since, the English have preferred not even to threaten to employ, let alone actually to practice, extreme measures. Compromise was to be sanctified in England by her experience with revolution in the seventeenth century, and no amount of contempt on the part of extremists can undo what was then achieved. That is why the Tudor age matters profoundly to modern England. It was through the experience of that age, with all its defects, that the country passed safely through its revolutionary epoch in the next century, for it was an apprenticeship in order, discipline, and a certain degree of self-government.

The Tudors worked with, and through, the people who mattered, taking them into partnership and evolving a truly governing class, which has sometimes been glibly called the gentry. Although the main lines of policy were laid down by the king or queen in council, and ratified by parliament, the day-to-day work was done by the officer who has been well described as the "Tudor maid-of-all-work," the justice of the peace. This office—first formulated in the twelfth century—was in effect an unpaid magistracy recruited from the lesser landowners, upon whom the routine work of government rested. The officers administered justice in most minor offenses, and they also administered the Poor Law, maintained the roads, and generally preserved the peace. It was their duty, too, to assess wages according to plenty and scarcity. It was always difficult to secure their cooperation in the enforcement of legislation that injured their interests—"antienclosure laws" for example. They were, however, for the most part valuable servants of the Crown just because they had a personal interest in the peace and wellbeing of their own neighborhood. The secret of the all-round success of Tudor government was that it rested upon this identity of interests. In

*Henry VIII rejects Roman Catholicism and founds the Church of England*

nearly all his multifarious duties the justice of the peace was doing his own business as a landlord. When this was not the case he could and generally did drag his feet. Then it was possible to keep him up to the mark by summoning him before the Star Chamber, but this was not often necessary. This happy combination of central strength and local interest preserved English government from either fatty degeneration of the heart on the one hand or hardening of the arteries on the other.

The central experience of the country in the sixteenth century was the breach with Rome, and it is from this that most of the greatness and success of modern England has arisen. The monarchy had kept the bishop of Rome at arm's length throughout most of the Middle Ages, when everywhere in Europe papal Rome seemed to be on the way to enjoying the imperial authority of the ancient Roman emperors. It was that very Tudor Englishman, Thomas Hobbes (born in 1588, the year of the Spanish Armada), who called the papacy "the ghost of the deceased Roman empire seated crowned on the grave thereof."

On the whole, however, the kings of England rejected the claims of the distant pope less fiercely than they did those of the archbishop of Canterbury who was close to home. They had done their best to keep the pope's hands off the property of their subjects, in which they had their own financial interest. And they had limited ecclesiastical jurisdiction, even at the cost of murdering Thomas Becket, the archbishop of Canterbury, in his own cathedral. By the sixteenth century, in fact, the authority of the Roman Church in England was already so far curtailed that the collapse of the clergy, their power, privileges, and property, before a royal assault resembled the fall of ripe fruit from a tree in a quite moderate wind. Henry VIII needed to do little more than give the tree an additional shake. The ripe fruit now consisted of the abbey lands, which were very rich and extensive, the monastic houses possessing about one third of the land of England. For generations the monks had grown fat on the gifts of the pious, and in large measure all that happened in 1536 when the monasteries were dissolved was that these benefactors resumed what had originally been their own. For long enough they had been used to referring to this or that monastic establishment as "my house." One may imagine the king shaking the tree in the midst of a circle of courtiers who caught the golden fruit as it fell and made themselves into a wealthier aristocracy. They were what the

*The Court of Wards, a prerogative tribunal established by Henry VIII*

 essayist Gilbert K. Chesterton called "the new grave lords that had eaten the abbeys' fruits, the men of the new religion with their bibles in their boots." Prominent among them were many families who were to figure largely in what became the "Whig oligarchy" in the next two centuries. It is not far from the truth to say that in despoiling the monasteries the king was building up the class which was to destroy him, which would replace monarchy with aristocracy or plutocracy.

Financial necessity has led to some desperate courses on the part of both individuals and nations. It would be too much to say that England, in the person of Henry VIII, broke with the papacy in order to rob the richest bank of the time. If this was what Henry did he might have made himself financially independent of parliamentary supply, much to the detriment of representative institutions—even to the point of their enfeeblement, as in France, or their disappearance, as in Spain. All the great nations of Europe had had such institutions during the Middle Ages, and all except England entered upon their modern history without them. Perhaps it would be better to say that the English acquired the habit of self-government because they acquired a parliament rather than that they acquired parliament because they had a talent for self-government.

Henry VIII was pursuing a typically Tudor policy when he took parliament into partnership in making his breach with the Roman Church. Not only were the rich implicated in the property grab, but the nation as a whole was required to accept the king's headship of the Church in England as a part of statute law. The penalties for denying it were enforced by the law of the land, and the change was made the less offensive because the forms of religious worship were only slightly altered, and altered very slowly. Henry VIII himself did not want change for the sake of change. He wanted to retain the outward forms of the old religion while repudiating the authority of the pope, who was throughout carefully called the bishop of Rome. All through this religious revolution sufficient emphasis was laid on the "foreign" nature of the Roman Catholic religion and the "usurped" nature of papal authority. England was "contracting" upon her insularity: that was the inward meaning of the term now used in statute to describe the island power. As the preamble of the Act of Restraint of Appeals (1533) put it: "by divers sundry old authentic histories and chronicles it is manifestly declared and expressed that this realm of England is an empire. . . ." Which simply meant that no power on earth was above it or above its king. That is precisely what Henry wanted to believe and have his people believe, so that he could put away his first wife, Catherine of Aragon, and marry Anne Boleyn, who, he had reason to believe, would produce for him a male heir to the throne (the heir which, in the event, turned out to be Elizabeth). He could do neither if the pope were master. Not only was divorce contrary to the law of the Roman Church, but the unfortunate Catherine was aunt to the Holy Roman Emperor, the pope's partner, so to speak, at the head of Christian Europe. One way or another Henry VIII had to repudiate papal authority and run his "empire" without acknowledging any superior. That was what his celebrated breach with Rome achieved.

The breach has been called a revolution, and the term is not extravagant. It set up, even if it did not create, the nation-state which is modern England, and the king's minister who carried through its establishment with almost diabolical skill was Thomas Cromwell. Cromwell's master, Thomas Wolsey, was an Ipswich butcher's son who rose through the Church to become lord chancellor, and the last of England's great ecclesiastical statesmen. Wolsey was described by a contemporary as the "proudest prelate that ever breathed," and certainly he lived on a scale seldom matched in that age; he kept a thousand servants, his palaces were more splendid than the king's, and for a decade and a half he held in his hands an accumulation of power rarely if ever equaled in England. While Henry VIII enjoyed himself, his chancellor Wolsey ran the realm; and under him the goal of English foreign policy first became defined as the balance of power on the Continent. Then Henry tired of Wolsey, who fell from favor, died disgraced, and was succeeded by Thomas Cromwell, son of a blacksmith who kept a public house at Putney. In his turn, Cromwell was the first great secular servant of the state. The revolution we associate with his name was not the reform of English religion but the rejection of papal authority. It was quite literally a revolution in government.

There were two other men called Thomas who rose to great eminence in Tudor administration, seeming to suggest that Napoleon's formula of a "career open to talent" existed in England some three centuries earlier than it did in France. There was Thomas More, who

also served as lord chancellor before he lost his head and (some believe) won a martyr's crown by refusing to accept the king's headship of the Church in England; "a man for all seasons," who wrote *Utopia,* a portrait of an ideal commonwealth. And there was Thomas Cranmer who served Henry as archbishop of Canterbury and was burned at the stake under Queen Mary, although he had assured himself of immortality by the Prayer Book for which he had been responsible in the previous reign. It is well to remember the brilliance of English literature as represented in the prose of that magnificent book. It is no less pertinent to associate the great flowering of the English language at this time with the release of spiritual energies by the Reformation.

The Reformation followed the breach with Rome. Religious worship

*Mary Queen of Scots, with crucifix in hand, kneels upon the scaffold before her executioner at Fotheringay Castle.*

became simpler and more adult and less repetitive; prayer became more concerned with adoration and less with petition; parson and congregation were in future less apt to be described as "God botherers" than as partners in personal communion with the Almighty. Luther had gone to the length of preaching "the priesthood of all believers," and in Elizabeth's reign the left-wing element in the English Church was already producing such presumptuous and schismatic persons as Henry Barrow and John Greenwood who called themselves Independents, holding out such dangerous doctrines as "every elder, though he be no doctor or pastor, is a bishop," and "set prayer is blasphemous." Such extreme doctrines savored of religious democracy and were extremely upsetting to the hierarchy. The queen herself, who took stern measures against the left wing, said she would not tolerate "newfangledness." The men who were already carrying Protestantism to such lengths were the first generation of what were to be America's Pilgrim Fathers. They had not yet made old England too hot for themselves, but it was not long before they imagined that life would be safer elsewhere. They were forebears of the men who, in the revolt of the American colonies, as the statesman Edmund Burke said, stood for "the dissidence of dissent and the Protestantism of the Protestant religion." It was thus that extreme Protestantism assisted the growth of democracy, which was to spread from church to state.

Elizabeth's abhorrence of the Puritan position, which smacked of religious republicanism, might have been expected to throw her into sympathetic alliance with the Queen of Scots, who was driven from her throne by the revolt of her Calvinistic subjects, who denounced her as the "Scarlet Woman." In fact, John Knox and the Kirk of Scotland preached against both queens as examples of the "monstrous regiment of women." Perhaps things would have been different if Mary had not pressed her claim to the throne of England. Driven from Scotland, the beautiful princess threw herself on her "sweet cousin of England" for succor. Elizabeth shut her up in "honorable captivity" in various English houses for the rest of her days. In 1587, not many months before Philip of Spain launched the Armada to rescue her and place her on the throne of England, Elizabeth felt compelled to end Mary's life as an intolerable menace. As long as Mary Queen of Scots lived to serve as the center of Catholic plots against the "Heretic Queen" of England, neither Elizabeth nor her realm were safe from murder and revolution. The fact that Mary was called the "honeypot" sweetened her not at all to the red-wigged and raddled English queen. Elizabeth did a bold, and perhaps a brutal, thing in putting her to death at Fotheringay, but it was, as Oliver Cromwell was to say when he did the same to the Queen of Scots' grandson Charles I, "cruel necessity." Anyway, Elizabeth managed to look the other way until the deed was done, and like a true daughter of her house she saw to it that her secretary, Davison, took the rap for the execution of Mary's death warrant.

There had been a strain of primitive communism in the social unrest of the later Middle Ages. John Ball, a peasant leader in the Peasants' Revolt, is chiefly remembered for having asked the question:

*When Adam delved and Eve span,*
*Who was then a gentleman?*

The nearest thing to a peasants' revolt under the Tudors was the Norfolk Furies of 1549, when large numbers of the rural population of East Anglia rose under Robert Kett, a tanner, and his brother. The interesting thing about Kett is that he called himself the King's Lieutenant and his encampment on Mousehold Heath above Norwich the King's Camp. In an age of king worship perhaps this was not surprising. The rebel leaders, like peasant leaders in other lands, notably old Russia, claimed only to be doing the justice that the king himself would have done if he had not been in the hands of wicked courtiers and greedy landlords. The king at that time was Edward VI, a boy of eleven and the only child of Henry VIII and Jane Seymour. Perhaps if he had been another Richard II he might have ridden out to lead and pacify them. Instead, Robert Kett's men slew the sheep, which, they held, were eating up their livelihood. "Enclosing landlords" were the villains of the piece all over the sheep-grazing lands of Tudor England. The poor men with Kett roasted the sheep at their campfires, and a good time was had by all until the king's soldiers with a stiffening of Switzers, or German mercenaries, descended on them and after a pitched battle put down the revolt which had held the city of Norwich and all eastern England in terror for many days. The Kett brothers were hanged, one on his own church tower at Wymondham and the other on the keep of Norwich Castle. (Henry VIII, dealing with a somewhat

*Queen Elizabeth I as a middle-aged monarch in a portrait of 1592*

*Sheepshearing scenes became increasingly common on the English landscape after the enclosure of arable farm lands.*

similar rising in the north of England in 1536, had only contrived to suppress it by treacherously turning upon the complainants and slaughtering them in large numbers after pretending to treat with them. That shameful affair was known as the Pilgrimage of Grace and was largely sparked off by the dissolution of the monasteries in the northern counties where they had done much for the relief of the poor.)

The hoof of the sheep, it was said, turned sand into gold, and the enclosure of arable, and common, land for sheep keeping was widely held responsible for social distress. There was, however, a steep price rise in the Tudor century, principally as a result of the flooding of Europe with silver from America, but in part due to the depreciation of the currency by Henry VIII. As always in such circumstances it was the fixed-income groups that chiefly suffered, those who had most difficulty in increasing their incomes in order to cope with higher prices. Enclosing land for the profitable pursuit of sheep farming was tempting for such people, for sheep farming was economical in labor costs. But it also created unemployment, and the argument that much land was now being put to its best use did not mollify men out of work.

The fact that the landowners were seeking to restore their fortunes in a time of acute inflation, which hit them with disproportionate severity, exempted them not a whit from bitter social protest and blame. The alarm created by beggary was echoed in the old nursery rhyme:

*Hark, hark, the dogs do bark,*
*The beggars are coming to town . . .*

and it is hardly an exaggeration to say that Tudor England went in terror of the tramp. The state had neither the will nor the means to tackle the problems of poverty and unemployment. Such problems were generally considered to be the concern of local authorities, towns, guilds, and private charity. Central government only paid serious attention to these matters when they gave rise to disturbances affecting the public order and the keeping of the peace. Many acts were passed to discourage enclosure, especially when it caused unemployment, but the lesser gentry who, as justices of the peace, were supposed to enforce them were also the people who were most anxious to be left alone to enclose. They could, however, be relied on to deal with the resulting poverty, especially when it occasioned disorder. The Elizabethan Poor

OVERLEAF: *a detail from a painting by Hendrick Cornelisz Vroom shows English and Spanish sailors hurling insults and firing at one another.*

Law, whose operation they were supposed to supervise, was very largely a peace-keeping measure, and it lasted with minor changes for more than two hundred years. What it amounted to was that the Tudors made a proper distinction between the rogue and the tramp, on the one hand, and the genuinely destitute and needy on the other. Their legislation provided for the apprenticeship of children of the poor, the imposition of a poor tax, and the appointment of overseers of the poor—all steps that marked a transition from voluntary to compulsory contribution. Even so, of course, the voluntary principle remained in a tradition of private generosity and personal service which runs like a golden thread through local government, in particular. The other legislative measure which comprised the labor code was the Statute of Laborers and Apprentices of 1563, which concerned what we would call industrial training and the regulation of the wages of skilled craftsmen. The latter aspect of it was to last until the nineteenth century, imposing still more tasks on the much-burdened justice of the peace.

Elizabethan England was for long enough, and at least until the Battle of Britain in 1940, regarded by the English people as their "finest hour." It was the hour of the Elizabethan theater, of the first attempts to colonize Virginia, of the Elizabethan sea dogs; an hour of great and glowing figures, like the Virgin Queen, indeed, who liked to acclaim herself as "mere English," and Walter Raleigh with his cloak and his potatoes and his tobacco, and Sir Philip Sidney, that flower of knightly self-abnegation, putting aside his glass of water for the relief of a comrade in battle; of great houses like Hardwick, of splendid palaces like Hampton Court, not to mention Wollaton Hall, that ornate and pretentious chateau outside Nottingham.

The remarkable woman under whom this outburst of energy and achievement occurred had a capacity for inspiring devotion unequaled among British monarchs. Her commanding presence, eloquence, and auburn hair proclaimed her the daughter of Henry VIII; she enjoyed her father's physical energy, courage, wilfulness, and resolution as well as his love for the chase, music, and dancing, and his talent for languages. One of her most precious inheritances, however, was Henry's effective fleet of fighting ships, which had saved him and would save her as they systematically defied the Catholic powers of Europe.

Elizabeth had a talent for watching a situation closely, calculating the odds, and making use of the contending forces where there was profit to be made. And profit in plenty was a motive underlying the unrelenting exploration and warfare of that age. In its pursuit Elizabeth skilfully abetted the attacks on Spain's ships and colonies in the New World by Francis Drake, John Hawkins, and other sea dogs; it was an activity through which the Crown might share in both the plunder and the resulting embarrassment of Spain. In 1580 Drake entered Plymouth Sound after an absence of nearly three years, during which time he had preyed on Spanish shipping and sailed around the globe, and there was high significance in the queen's act of knighting him soon afterward on the deck of his ship, the *Golden Hind.* By doing so, she issued a direct challenge to the king of Spain, while appealing to her subjects to look to the sea for their strength. Simultaneously while she was encouraging her seamen to singe the Spanish king's beard and make away with his treasure ships like licensed pirates, she went through the motions of negotiating a French alliance. Procrastination, an air of innocence, many fair words and not a few politic lies, an occasional apology, a constant and careful shifting of her weight on the scales of the European balance of power to protect the interests of her country—she did anything and everything to fend off enemies with whom she did not wish, and could not afford, to come to open war. Without declaring war on Spain, she—through her seamen and God's winds—achieved the impossible in 1588 by defeating the great armada sent by Philip II to conquer England. Combining the royal navy with armed merchant ships, the English under Lord Howard assembled a fleet that approximated that of the Spanish; harrying the foe with artillery fire, dispersing them with fire ships, the English forced the Spanish to abandon their invasion attempt. As Lord Howard described the event, scarcely realizing the magnitude of his achievement, "Their force is wonderful great and strong, yet we pluck their feathers by little and little." At last, running before a storm, the Armada sailed north around Scotland and Ireland, suffering terribly from gales and a shortage of water and food, and at last reached the coast of Spain with only half the fleet that had set sail so confidently for England. To the English seamen, who had lost not a single ship, and to the people who had been spared invasion, it seemed a miracle. By the last decade and a half of her reign, Elizabeth had achieved her inexpensive glory, and her people were beginning to breathe more freely than they had earlier.

All through the century which culminated in the triumphs of Elizabeth, significant economic and social changes had been taking place quietly in the body of society. In agriculture, large-scale enterprise was evident in the enclosure of more and more land for sheep raising, with crop farming being run increasingly on "business" lines. At least one result was that the medieval rural scene, with the barnyard life going on immediately outside the window, was giving way to a scene of hedged fields, or "closes," and urban-style houses in a country setting. The coal industry had begun its first great expansion; investors were beginning to risk large amounts of capital in domestic ventures.

Like all great peoples in whom the blood flows hot and strong, the Elizabethan English had their own species of vulgarity. The men dressed in all the colors of the peacock, and the women bared their bosoms in a manner that on occasion outdid anything that the fashions of the twentieth century have done thus far. The age and the realm were at last sufficiently safe to turn the fortified manor house into a toy, retaining battlements that were never meant for battle, moats that were dry, and arrow-slits altered to become wide casements. Before the age ended, Richard Hooker had set the Anglican Church to music in the sonorities of his *Laws of Ecclesiastical Polity,* and within ten years of Elizabeth's death was to appear the matchless prose of King James' Authorized Version of the Bible which was, strange to say, the work of a committee.

Beneath all the rhetoric and the swagger, behind all the pomp and panoply which swell and sing to breaking point in the Elizabethan style in poetry and stone, there sounds for the first time the measured rhythm of the civilian life, the kind of life that men live when they are not in the theater or in court dress, at Bankside or Nonsuch or Greenwich palace. Then one sees them going about a peaceful world in the broadcloth of Samuel Pepys instead of the gorgeous trappings of Sir Walter Raleigh, doing their bookkeeping by double entry, traveling with one servant and a portmanteau instead of a posse of armed retainers, sleeping between walls of wainscot instead of tapestry, with Dutch gables overhead instead of an embattled parapet. The Englishman's house was no doubt still his castle, but the crenelation and the loopholes were becoming vestigial, fashionable survivals in a largely civilian world.

*A version of Cornelis Visscher's famous view of Elizabethan London includes this detail of the bustle and congestion around London Bridge.*

CHAPTER V

# CIVIL WAR AND DICTATORSHIP

When Elizabeth died in 1603 she was succeeded by the only son of Mary Queen of Scots, King James VI of Scotland, who ascended the English throne as James I. The first of the Stuart rulers, he was a conceited, garrulous man, a scholar with little knowledge of men, a Scotsman with little understanding of England. He had a horror of violence and no regard for sea power, so he allowed the great navy of Henry VIII and Elizabeth to decay, and was consequently unable to back up his foreign policy. In the process he also incurred the deep resentment of English mariners and merchants for the house of Stuart. His reign was dominated by a political struggle between king and parliament for authority in government, and before his death in 1625 that struggle had become acute. Under his son Charles I it culminated in civil war, in the course of which that unfortunate king literally lost his head to the executioner in 1649.

The civil war of the seventeenth century, and the dictatorship of Oliver Cromwell that followed, form the central experience of English history. The war began in 1642 and lasted, in two phases, for seven years; it was the last time that Englishmen took up arms against each

*Hardwick Hall, the climax of Elizabethan Renaissance design*

other. They were reluctant to begin it, they never ceased to attempt negotiation while it went on, and they sheathed their swords briskly when it was over. Then, having tried the king for starting it and executing him, they proceeded to quarrel among themselves, and finally decided to recall the Prince of Wales from exile to the throne. Since then there has always been a king or queen of England.

Having chopped off their king's head somewhat more than a hundred years before the Americans ended another English king's power on the other side of the Atlantic, and more than a century before the French sent their monarch to the guillotine, the English felt that they had had enough of extreme courses, and they have managed to go in for compromise ever since. As his Grace the duke of Devonshire once told a Frenchwoman who asked him why democratic institutions always seemed to work so much more smoothly in England than in France: "Madame, the reason is quite obvious. We cut off our king's head a hundred and forty-four years before you did yours." The English did not want the civil war to begin, and since that time they have been even more determined that there should never be another. Having a politically adroit governing class, and a good deal of skepticism about issues that are worth fighting for, let alone dying for, they have got along, ignobly perhaps, but certainly with decency, and without much internal bloodletting ever since. When it comes to heroics they prefer Nelson to Cromwell.

It might be best to say that the English went to war with each other owing to a breakdown of statesmanship, and a total lack of rapport between king and Commons. Charles I was a short, bandy-legged man who spoke with a stammer, looked well on horseback (and therefore he was pleased when he was painted that way), and was the very model of a gentleman. Devout, circumspect, and scholarly, he acquired the habit of reproaching the House of Commons in the tone of a long-suffering schoolmaster. The trouble with this was that the Commons and the men who dominated it had undergone a vast change. By Charles I's day, self-government had become a habit in England, and the men who had made it a reality were the country gentlemen who sat in the House of Commons. Deputy lieutenants, sheriffs, justices of the peace, royal commissioners—they were men who had done well on the land and who possessed money and real political ability, acquired

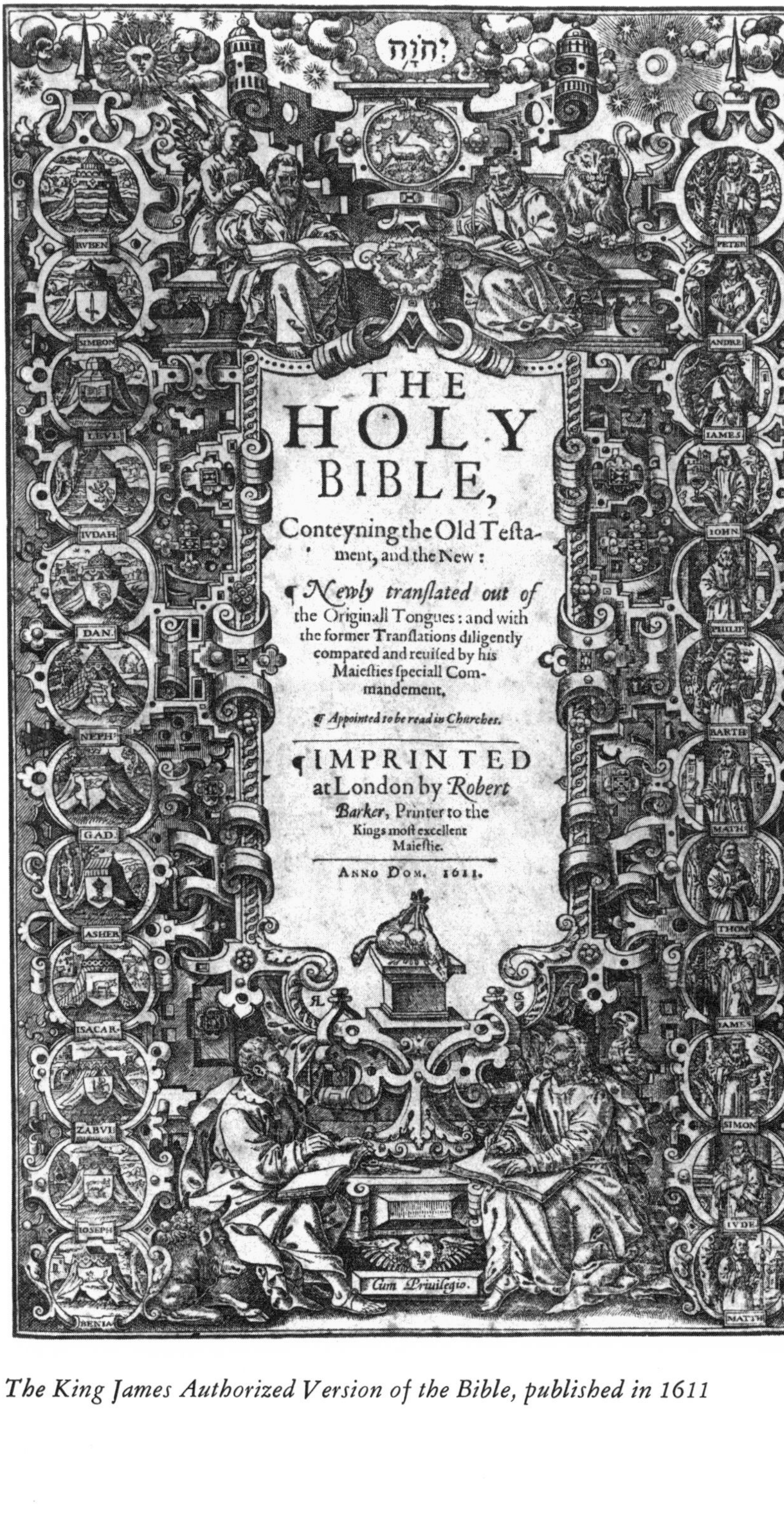


*The King James Authorized Version of the Bible, published in 1611*

through years of practical experience. Men of business educated in the market place, on the bench, or at the universities, they were by now accustomed to conducting government affairs on a daily basis. Once the threat of the Armada had passed, these country gentlemen were able to breathe easier, and began to be more critical of the way England's affairs were managed. This attitude was only heightened by the Stuart kings' personal ineptitude and their habit of bestowing royal patronage on unpopular men. Their quarrel with the Crown was sharpened further by divergent religious views. A great change had taken place in England with the Reformation, and people were turning ever more to the Puritan preacher and the prayer meeting, and away from anything that had the outward appearance of popery. (It has been said that Queen Elizabeth's one serious mistake was in not providing the Church with preachers, for neither she nor her Stuart successors ever grasped the passion of their people for sermons—preferably long ones.) The breach between court and country that had been evident in the time of Elizabeth widened considerably as a result of the disreputability of James I's court, and when Charles I came to the throne, a real gulf existed between these two profoundly different ways of life. The country gentlemen, alienated by the Stuarts, turned their talents to active opposition to the monarchy.

When Charles I's favorite, the duke of Buckingham—who had been responsible for a series of disastrous foreign adventures—was murdered, the act turned the king away from his subjects and enforced his determination to rule without the parliament he had come to hate. For eleven years, no parliament sat. When elections were again held, in the autumn of 1640, it was not the English, curiously enough, but the Scots who forced the event. In attempting to impose the Church of England's Prayer Book on the Scots while he was trying, in England, to get along without parliament, Charles I outraged both countries simultaneously and ended by losing his power in both places. The Scots not only refused to adopt the Prayer Book; they drew up a National Covenant which described the liturgy of the English Church as blasphemous and a creature of popery, and they swore to live and die in their own religion. Scottish armies occupied Northumberland and Durham, demanding money as their price of withdrawal, and the king's peers were forced to advise him to call a parliament. The one that convened—

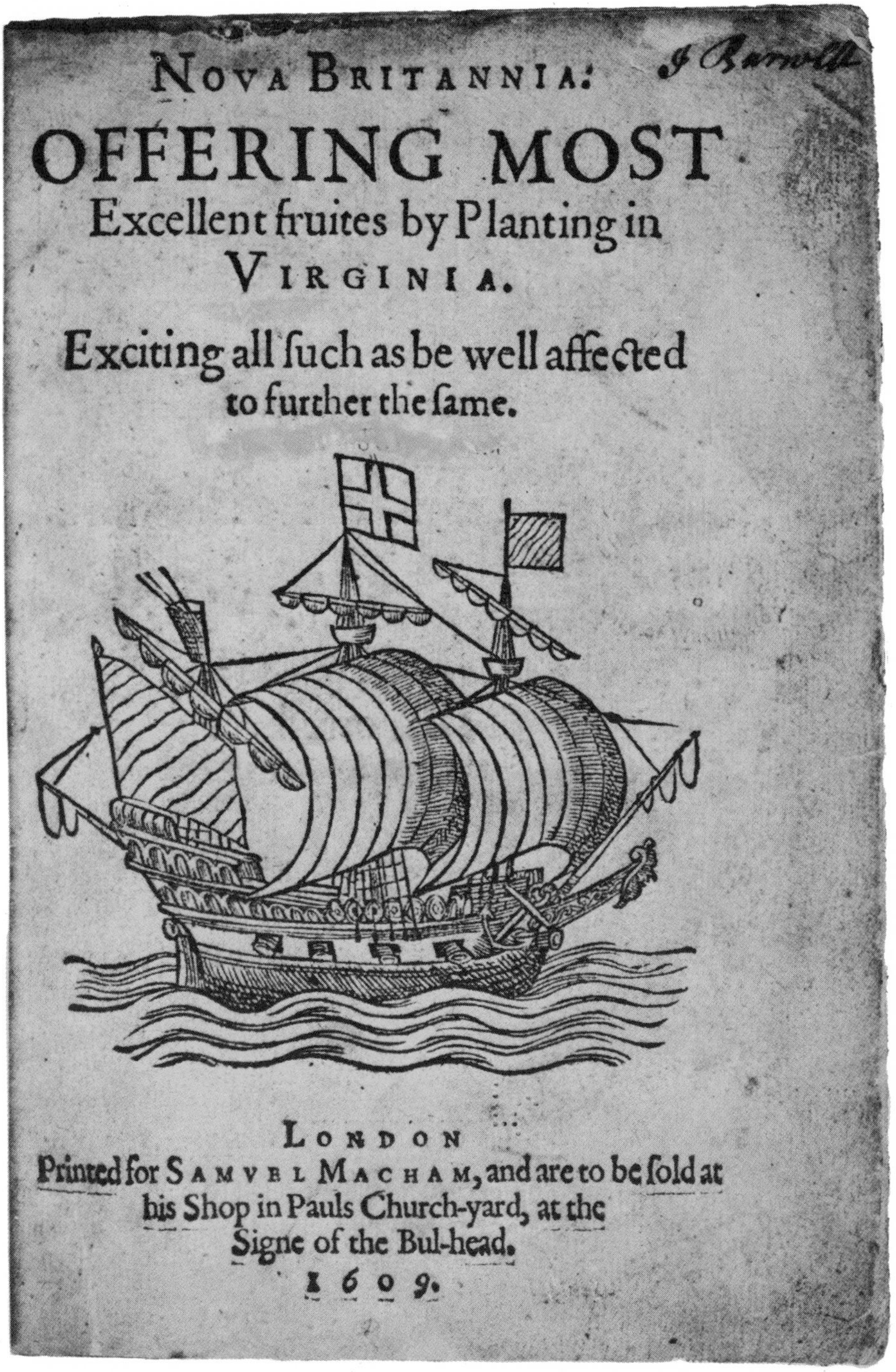

NOVA BRITANNIA:

OFFERING MOST

Excellent fruites by Planting in

VIRGINIA.

Exciting all ſuch as be well affected

to further the ſame.

LONDON

Printed for SAMVEL MACHAM, and are to be ſold at

his Shop in Pauls Church-yard, at the

Signe of the Bul-head.

1609.

*The title page from an emigration tract of 1609 by Robert Johnson*

known as the Long Parliament—was to endure for thirteen years and carry out a revolution. 

Before the civil war began, the king had surrendered on every important political question. Step by step, statute by statute, the Long Parliament (1640–53) took away the bones of contention: Star Chamber, taxation without consent, intermission of parliament. All that remained was the matter of religion, and in that day and age religion was everything. The king would die for the Church of England; large numbers of Englishmen were ready to die to rid themselves of it; and since the king was its head, toppling the Church meant toppling the Crown. Such was the perilous legacy of the breach with Rome and the establishment of the royal supremacy. Viewed from Rome, it may well have appeared that the chickens were coming home to roost.

It was, of course, during the reign of Charles I that the great migration of Protestants—and some Catholics—to America took place, to lay the foundations of empire in the New World. The adventuresome Elizabethans had shown the way; now that there were pressing reasons to go, there was a large-scale exodus, particularly from the southeast of England. Of some twenty-five thousand English who had settled in New England by 1640, it is estimated that two thirds or more came from the counties of the southeast and from the Midlands; accustomed there to large villages, they naturally took the notion of the township with them across the Atlantic, where it left a profound imprint on the new land. Many émigrés went to Virginia, or Bermuda, or to the West Indies. Nonconformists for the most part, who had been persecuted by Charles I's archbishop of Canterbury, William Laud, they sought a home where they could lead the religious life of their own choosing; and while free land or the lure of adventure or dreams of wealth may have played some part in attracting them to America, it is interesting to note that the great tide of migration virtually came to a halt when religious persecution in England ceased about 1640. Charles I could only have been happy to be rid of these pesky, potentially dangerous folk; on the Continent the savage results of religious disputes were all too evident. The Thirty Years' War was raging in Europe. From 1618 to 1648 on the Continent Catholic and Protestant cut each other's throats or blew each other's brains out with little intermission. It was an ideological conflict, which meant that neither side could sheathe the

*Sir Anthony Van Dyck's portrait of Charles I depicts the king, cavalierly clad, as usual, in equestrian attire.*

 sword until the achievement of total victory or the suffering of total defeat. This kind of war was always repellent to the English, it being inimical to compromise and common sense. They prefer to fight limited liability wars, or wars for limited objectives, so that the contestants can quit their fighting when it doesn't seem worthwhile going on, thus living to fight another day. Lewis Carroll made the point in *Through the Looking Glass:* "What's the time now?" Tweedledee looked at his watch and said: "Half-past four." "Let's fight till six and then have dinner," said Tweedledum.

The English civil wars of the seventeenth century scarcely belong at all to the European religious wars of that age. They might be described as conflicts in which the squirearchy, acting in concert with the merchant interests, struck down the royal power, as Trevelyan put it, "in a series of quarrels of which the chief motive was religious and the chief result political." It would be a mistake to attempt to pigeonhole the king's followers or their opponents in neat categories, but it may be said in general that the older aristocratic group—a majority of the nobles and squires of ancient lineage, especially those in the north and west who were farthest from the capital—tended to side with the Crown; while the "new men"—squires connected with the mercantile community, Londoners, and men from the trading centers of the south and east—were likely to oppose the king. Social class rarely determined on which side a man would fight, though commercial interest certainly gave the parliamentary cause predominance in the urban centers. Most often what settled a man's loyalty was his religion. Generally, but not always, the loyal Anglican was the loyal royalist, while most men of Puritan persuasion went with the parliament. And of course local affiliations counted for much. A great figure like the duke of Newcastle in the north could influence the loyalty of thousands. Nor should we forget the words of Edward Hyde, Lord Clarendon, who saw the war at close quarters and wrote that "the number of those who desired to sit still was greater than those who desired to engage in either party." Many men's instinctive loyalties were like those of Sir Edmund Verney, the king's standardbearer, who said, "I have eaten the king's bread . . . and I will not do so base a thing as to forsake him," even though, like Verney, they may have disapproved his every action.

The war seesawed back and forth, and after 1645, when parliament established the New Model Army, the fighting began to take on an ideological character, largely because of the religious fervor of Oliver Cromwell and many of his troops. When this happened, it produced the few examples of atrocity, as when Sir Thomas Fairfax, the parliamentarian commander—exasperated when his forces were held up for many crucial days in the siege of Colchester Castle—had the two royalist officers, Lucas and Lisle, shot after their surrender. It was an action so shocking that memorial statues to the pair were raised at the site of their death. There were other examples: where the extremes of Catholic or Puritan feeling came into collision, as at Bolton; or where a long siege and the prospect of very rich plunder led to incredibly savage fighting and indiscriminate killing, as at Basing House near Oxford. But more typical of the war was the message sent by Sir William Waller, member of parliament, and parliamentarian commander in Gloucestershire, to his royalist opposite number before a battle: "My affections," he wrote to the fellow soldier whom he had known well in happier days, "are so unchangeable that hostility itself cannot violate my friendship. We are both upon the stage, and we must act the parts assigned to us in this tragedy. Let us do it in a way of honor and without personal animosities." A war between two small minorities of gentlemen could, and mostly did, remain a gentlemanly war. To the contestants in Europe's Thirty Years' War it must have seemed little more than a family tiff.

The opponents fought generally by "push of pike" and, as one officer complained, "I cannot conceive what these fellows are doing with their weapons," for some of them would use their pikes to pull down ripe fruit or to hook clean linen off clotheslines or to split faggots. The weather, too, was typically English: wild winds in August, mild and foggy winters, plenty of rain at all times. Punches were frequently pulled, and one contingent of Frenchmen who had come over to fight for the king found that they had been fighting for the parliament. Instead of uniforms, for identification the two sides generally wore different colored scarves over their mufti. There was a good deal of incompetence on both sides. After two years of war it became evident that the parliamentary forces—despite one important victory—lacked the organization and the military leadership to win decisively, so the New Model Army was created to remedy matters. Regularly fed and

*An eyewitness rendering of the regicide of Charles I depicts onlookers, except for the swooning lady in the foreground, raptly viewing the grisly event.*

more or less regularly paid, the "Saints" who served in it were better disciplined than the disorganized, wrangling, nearly bankrupt "Cavaliers" who opposed them. Both sides underwent a curious change, as one of Charles I's men wrote: "Those under the King's commanders grew insensibly into all the licence, disorder and impiety with which they had reproached the rebels; and they again into great discipline, diligence and sobriety; which begat courage and resolution in them, and notable dexterity in achievements and enterprises. [In this way] one side seemed to fight for monarchy with the weapons of confusion, and the other to destroy the King and government with all the principles and regularity of monarchy." There were also to be many occasions when it looked as if the English were prepared to fight until the last drop of Scottish blood had been shed, for, like so much in English history, the outcome of the war depended upon the Scots, who had also had much to do with its beginning. Charles I had tried to compel them to worship according to his Anglican Prayer Book, but the Scots had signed the National Covenant to stand by their own Calvinist brand of Protestantism. After the king had been at war with his subjects for a year, the Scots came in on the side of parliament, and in 1646 the fighting ended with the king in the hands of the Scots and willing to sign the covenant himself, or anything else that would give him an army to win back what he had lost. It was this bargain that made the second civil war certain and earned him the title the Man of Blood from his enemies.

In 1647 the king fell into the hands of parliament and then was seized by the army, which by now was suspicious of both king and parliament. Charles was tried and convicted of treason for levying war against parliament, and on January 30, 1649, he was beheaded. Once his head was off, he went into the future as Charles the Martyr, the king who died for the Church of England. A church which owed its salvation to such a double-dealer may have needed no less than the shedding of royal blood to give it sanctity; at any rate, it has lasted ever since. At the time, however, it was considerably populated by clergymen like the celebrated vicar of Bray, a parson of changeable views who was immortalized by the line of an anonymous eighteenth-century song; "Whatsover King shall reign, I will be the Vicar of Bray, Sir!" Perhaps this gentleman's flexibility was not inappropriate to the servant of a communion whose head (the Lord's Anointed) was King Charles II, a flexible character if ever there was one.

"Historically," one authority has written, "the Commonwealth is so much time wasted. Its only consequence was the reaction it inspired, and the party divisions it consolidated." Perhaps it would be better to emphasize the educational value of the attempt to live without the traditional institutions of a monarchy and a bicameral legislature. After all, it is never altogether without value to a nation's historical experience to have gone as far as possible toward a total break with traditional loyalties. There is much to be said, in terms of political statistics, for having gone to the limit, at least once. Henceforth the temptation to venture so far into the unknown is hardly likely to hold much attraction.

Apart from the salutary lessons to be learned from extremism and from the consequent reaction thereto, the years of the interregnum—the period officially known as the Commonwealth, when England tried to live without a king—created a tradition of what might fairly be called left-wing politics. Even while the king was still alive, the victorious army of the parliament—officers and men—held a series of debates in the parish church at Putney, in London, to discuss the future government of England. This was in the autumn of 1647 when it seemed certain that England would be confronted with some form of democracy, although that word was not used. Those debates have come down to us almost verbatim, and the record presents an astonishing picture of the rich fabric of English political thinking in that astonishing age. We hear the words not only of the officers ("grandees," they are called)—such men as Oliver Cromwell and his son-in-law Henry Ireton—but also of noncommissioned officers and ordinary troopers, men who in the record are simply called buffcoat or trooper. An extraordinary thing had happened, for the rank and file were sitting down to thrash out their differences with the officers. "There are many thousands of us soldiers that have ventured our lives," Trooper Sexby said; "we have little propriety in the kingdom as to our estates, yet we have had a birthright." Suspecting that Cromwell and some of the others might be thinking of their position in a new peerage under a restored king, another man wondered "what the soldier hath fought for all this while," and was concerned lest "he hath fought to enslave himself, to give power to men of riches, men of estates, to make him a perpetual slave." Such men as these had no intention of being deprived of the fruits of their hardships and their victories. It was one Colonel Rainsborough, who achieved immortality for these otherwise faceless men by delivering what has been described as "the straightest and simplest claim for equality ever made in English history." "Really," he said, "I think that the poorest he that is in England hath a life to live as the greatest he; and therefore truly, Sir, I think it's clear that every man that is to live under a government ought first by his own consent to put himself under that government; and I do think that the poorest man in England is not at all bound in a strict sense to that government that he hath not had a voice to put himself under; insomuch that I should doubt whether he was an Englishman." Call it chauvinistic, if we will, it speaks volumes for the proud self-confidence of the men of Cromwell's army that the colonel added those last words. They remind one of another proud and peerless patriot, John Milton—Cromwell's supporter and pamphleteer—who held that when God bethinks himself of any new thing by way of reformation, He imparts it first to His Englishmen. Thus Wordsworth, two centuries later, spoke of his country teaching nations how to live.

What cardinal features of modern England were established by the civil war and the settlement that followed? The chief of these was the parliamentary monarchy that was secured once and for all. Charles I had gone to his death declaring that "a sovereign and a subject are clean different things," but the English Revolution of the Stuart century prepared the way for the acceptance of the view which was best expressed a hundred years later by Jean Jacques Rousseau that "the people compose the sovereign, which is the essential meaning of democracy." Before that term came into common use, England had still to undergo her one and only experience of dictatorship, under the protectorate of Oliver Cromwell. The East Anglian country gentleman who governed England at the head of a victorious army from 1653 until his death in 1658 represented a singularly mild form of dictatorship, it is true. The Protector preferred to call himself "a good constable set to keep the peace of the parish," and said that he would have been glad "to have lived under my own woodside, to have kept a flock of sheep, rather than undertake such a government as this." Even before the civil war

*Lord Protector Oliver Cromwell keeps faction and war underfoot in this allegory of his absolute rule.*

 threw him up as a successful cavalry commander he had thought seriously more than once of going to America, where he would undoubtedly have become one of the Founding Fathers. In England his parliamentary experience had been that of a rather incoherent backbencher, and he was always to prove singularly inept in the arts of parliamentary management. So far as we know he played football when he was at Cambridge, and it is difficult to imagine him at cricket, the game with which parliamentary government is more often compared. To Cromwell, no branch of human affairs was ever to be conducted like a game, and politics to him, as to his medieval ancestors, was tributary to the bringing of the Kingdom of Heaven. He could, and did, fight a campaign with the bible and the sword, but parliamentary maneuver was vain expense in the eyes of God's Englishman. It was left to the Victorians to set up a statue of Cromwell at the entrance to the House of Commons, the institution which he had neither the skill nor the patience to govern.

When Cromwell, accompanied by thirty musketeers, went to the so-called Rump Parliament in April, 1653, and sent it packing, there remained in England no monarchy and no legislative body, and the Established Church was prostrate. The sole effective power in the state consisted of Oliver Cromwell and his troopers; for a time all the carefully nurtured constitutional safeguards built up over the centuries were abandoned, and England was ruled by one man's will. When Cromwell failed to govern through an ineffective successor to the Rump Parliament, he took the title of Lord Protector and resorted to a regime of major generals who ruled over eleven military districts. Cromwell was never to be forgiven for this resort to government by the major generals. The best reply to the common charge that he ruled by the sword has been said to be the fact that there was nothing else left to rule by. Nevertheless, the resentment remains, and such rule has never been attempted since. The very memory of it has had a salubrious effect. "No standing army in time of peace" was to become the favorite maxim of English government until, at the time of the French Revolution, the prime minister exclaimed impatiently, "as if a standing army in time of peace had not been kept on foot for above a century, or as if any danger to the liberties of the nation had ever risen from it." What has to be remembered, however, is that after the restoration of Charles

II in 1660 such an establishment existed on a strictly parliamentary basis: the Militia Act of 1661, and a series of Army Acts which had to be renewed annually. As a consequence of painful experience, the restoration of the king was statutorily accompanied by the restoration of a regularly elected parliament. The Triennial Act of 1664, requiring that not more than three years should elapse between the termination of one parliament and the holding of another, was not very effectual since the statute contained no teeth, and nothing really effective was achieved until after the Revolution of 1688. In all such matters of bringing pressure to bear on the executive the solution lay in the establishment of a workable parliamentary control of finance.

It was said of Cromwell that his greatness at home was but a shadow of his greatness abroad, and it is true that he made England's name feared and respected in Europe as it had never been since the days of Henry V, and was never to be again until the Pitts, father and son. The English poets, from Marvell to Milton, celebrated him exultantly. In the perspective of three centuries he looks at us down the vistas of time with the rugged face of a noble warrior. Today he is remembered as God's Englishman, the nation's typical heroic man in his strength and his weakness. He died on a night of terrible storm, as he had lived in his country's day of storm, crying out in his fear of "falling into the hands of the living God."

That same night another man, as yet a boy, was carrying out his first recorded experiment—in the force of the wind. Young Isaac Newton, the future founder of mathematical physics, was also a man of religion. He hoped that his great book, *Principles of Mathematics,* which appeared in 1687, only thirty years after the death of Cromwell, "might," as he said, "work with considering men for the belief of a deity." These two, Cromwell and Newton, were the greatest Englishmen of their century, and although they expressed two very different facets of their country and their age, they did not represent any basic antagonism. The greatest characteristic of the English mind in that century, often called the century of genius, was its fundamental unity.

CHAPTER VI

# WHIGS AND TORIES

When the Lord Protector died on September 3, 1658, he was succeeded by his eldest surviving son, Richard, who was to resign within a few months and be remembered only as Tumble-down Dick. Then General George Monck, a resolute patriot of the Cromwellian breed who commanded the army in Scotland, marched on London and declared for a free parliament, a luxury the country had not enjoyed for twenty years. A parliament was elected under Monck's protection, and its sole claim to historic memory is that it called back the eldest son of Charles I almost without conditions to serve as sovereign. In 1645, with the civil war well under way, the fifteen-year-old boy who was to become Charles II had been sent to safety in the west of England, whence he later fled to Europe. A decade and a half later, on May 25, 1660, through the intercession of parliament and General Monck, monarchy—stripped of much of its arbitrary power—was restored to England when the tall, swarthy Charles stepped ashore on Dover beach to be greeted with reverence by Monck and with unbridled enthusiasm by the immense crowd of Englishmen that cheered his triumphal passage along the road back to London.

*Saint Paul's Cathedral, rebuilt by Christopher Wren after the Great Fire*

In their joy at having a king again the people had forgotten all else. Charles II's proposed epitaph had not yet been invented:

*Here lies our sovereign lord the King*
*Whose word no man relies on,*
*Who never said a foolish thing*
*And never did a wise one.*

A gentleman's agreement is all very well between English gentlemen, but the Stuarts were half French, half Scottish, and wholly un-English. The only way to deal with them satisfactorily would have been to have everything down in black and white, signed and sealed; they were the very types for whom social contracts were invented. Charles II was a true grandson of that charming rascal, Henry IV of France, and his subtitle was the Merry Monarch, which he well deserved. He gave good value for money in terms of entertainment but the money was always running out, and to get more he was prepared to sell almost anything and everything, including his own foreign policy, the control of which was greatly coveted by his rich cousin, Louis XIV of France. Charles' idea of success was to get hold of enough money to make himself independent of parliament and to make love to every pretty woman he caught sight of. He pursued both aims for some twenty-five years, and his subjects enjoyed watching him. "So long as this world is this world," the economist Walter Bagehot once said, "will a buoyant life be the proper source of an animated Conservatism." Or, as that other humorist, Michael Finsbury, put it: "Nothing like a little judicious levity." Like most kings, Charles II was a conservative, and perhaps levity is the only way of making life tolerable when one's father has been executed. It was clear that more than the monarchy had been restored with Charles. The Church, which had in a sense never been away, came back with the king, and in 1660 bishops were permitted to resume their seats in the House of Lords, ecclesiastical courts took up their functions once again, and subsequently the Anglican parson and Prayer Book were restored to supremacy while dissenters were liable to be punished. (Paradoxically, both Charles II and his brother James II were responsible for preventing the Anglican Church from becoming as harsh an instrument of religious persecution as it might have been, by their Declarations of Indulgence to suspend the laws against nonconformists—paradoxically, that is, because both kings were almost certainly less concerned with the rights of their Protestant nonconformist subjects than with the privileges they sought for their coreligionists of the Catholic faith.) Despite several decades of intermittent oppression, much Protestant thought and practice managed nevertheless to become deeply ingrained in the English character; such habits as family prayer, Bible reading, and the Puritan Sunday—a day set aside for rest and meditation—survived.

One of the most significant events of the Restoration was the incorporation by Charles II of the Royal Society of London in 1662 "to promote the welfare of the arts and sciences." The scientific movement that flowered in the work of Isaac Newton came about through what one of its members, Robert Boyle, termed the Invisible College—a group of men who had been associating in London for philosophical discussions under the inspiration of Francis Bacon since the 1640s. The names of the first generation of Fellows of the Royal Society read like a roll call of the modern mind. There was Boyle, the father of modern chemistry; Sir William Petty, founder of population statistics; Dr. John Wilkins, bishop of Chester and brother-in-law of Oliver Cromwell, who published a treatise on the moon in 1638 and one called *Mathematical Magick* a decade later; Robert Hooke, the physicist, mathematician, and inventor, who was regarded as the greatest mechanic of his age; Christopher Wren, scientist and architect; and many others. Through such men as these the Royal Society separated "the knowledge of nature from the colours of rhetoric, the devices of fancy, or the delightful deceit of fables." It demanded of its members a "close, naked, natural way of speaking, . . . preferring the language of artisans, countrymen, and merchants before that of wits or scholars," thus drawing the line firmly between science and literature.

Although Charles II patronized the Society and built the Royal Observatory at Greenwich in 1675, he is probably better remembered for what he was than for what he did. It was said of him that he "minds nothing but his lust and hath taken ten times more care and pains in making friends between Lady Castlemaine and Mrs. Stewart, when they have fallen out, than ever he did to save his Kingdom." Mrs. Castlemaine and Louise de Kérouaille, his two principal mistresses, set a tone that made life at court a continuing scandal, and it was with a sense of some relief that the people learned of the king's taking as a mistress the actress and former orange seller, Nell Gwyn, who was roundly cheered in the streets as the Protestant Whore. To a people who had suffered under the stern discipline of the Saints, the rule of the sinners was greatly to be preferred. The theaters, which had been closed since 1642, reopened to present plays marked by wit, brilliance, and a moral outlook reflecting life at court. The maypole went up and the hearts of men delighted once again in their customary sins. Within the age of Charles II yet in no sense of it were John Bunyan, who published *Pilgrim's Progress* in 1678, and John Milton—blind and old in a world that had fallen in ruin about him—who brought out *Paradise Lost* in 1667.

England returned to the main, but neither straight nor narrow, path of her history, never again to depart from it. It is now more than three hundred years since the aberration which got rid of both church and king, setting up a commonwealth, or free state, and requiring every Englishman of the age of eighteen and over to take an oath of loyalty to the Commonwealth, which by law had neither king nor House of Lords. The monarchy had not simply been allowed to lapse: the office of king had been formally abolished by act of parliament, having been found "unnecessary, burdensome, dangerous to the liberty, safety, and public interest of the people." At his trial Charles I had said: "The Commons of England will not thank you for this change." The Commons of England had not been consulted for nearly ten years. Now, in 1660, they had been consulted at last, and he was proved right. They took Cromwell's body from the grave and stuck his head on Temple Bar like that of any common criminal, and they hacked up a handful of regicides; then they declared that all legislation since the death of Charles I was null and void. Charles II's Declaration of Breda gave the vaguest possible promise of a free pardon for all his subjects who had been in revolt; "a liberty to tender conscience," which meant no persecution for religious opinion; and (of course) "the full satisfaction of all arrears due to the officers and soldiers of the army under the command of General Monck." If there were to be any exceptions to the free pardon, the onus of naming them was put upon parliament. Charles II did his best to restrain vindictiveness; that trait, in any case, was not among his faults.

As might be expected, his reign was not to be one of peace and harmony, let alone of glory. In the dark days of 1665–67 it seemed at times that England's sun must be setting in a fiery pool of divine wrath. In 1665 the Plague, in what was its latest and greatest onslaught since the Black Death, turned London into a vast pest house. The following year the Great Fire of London destroyed everything between the Tower and the Temple. And in 1667 the Dutch, at the end of a war fought to settle the commercial rivalry between the two maritime powers, sailed into the Medway and burned a considerable portion of the royal navy. Yet even amid disaster there were signs of hope. The Great Fire at least accomplished a salutary if cruel cauterization. Large areas of rat-infested property were destroyed, clearing the ground for rebuilding the

*Assisted by quadrant and telescope, astronomers at the Royal Observatory chart heavenly bodies.*

*Sir Christopher Wren before his masterpiece, Saint Paul's Cathedral*

city in style. Regrettably the opportunity was lost, although some exciting plans were made and have survived. It was the age of Sir Christopher Wren, the country's greatest urban architect, and who can say what London might look like if his contemporaries' attachments to the old, existing buildings had not balked him? He had to be content instead to leave as his memorial the great church of Saint Paul (and more than fifty other lesser London churches). Nicholas Barbon did succeed in building some handsome town houses, presaging the famous Georgian phase of urban housebuilding. And following their sea war with the Dutch, the English were awarded, through the Treaty of Breda, the colonies of New York, New Jersey, and Delaware in America.

The poet John Dryden was to celebrate 1666 as *Annus Mirabilis,* the Year of Wonders, with special reference to the king's personal energy as a fire fighter and his care for his suffering subjects, although not even poetic license can quite convince us of "the pious tears which down his cheeks did shower," so that

*The wretched in his grief forgot his own,*
*So much the pity of a king has power . . .*

The next time the English found it necessary to get rid of their king it was even simpler, for practice makes perfect. James II, the younger brother and successor of Charles II, came to the throne in 1685, assuring his subjects that "I have often heretofore ventured my life in defense of this nation, and I shall go as far as any man in preserving it in all its just rights and liberties." But his public practice of the Catholic faith and his intolerable misgovernment soon disturbed the realm, and within a year the king had alienated most of his friends and greatly disquieted nearly everyone else. When it came to getting rid of James II, a group of his subjects actually left a boat for two nights in the Thames, and on the second night he took it, fleeing the country and taking his wife and baby boy, the Prince of Wales, to safety at the court of France. His son-in-law, William of Orange, Statholder of Holland, simply stepped into his shoes, having accepted a so-called Declaration of Rights drawn up in 1689, which parliament promptly made into a statute. This was the nearest thing England has ever had to a written constitution and not very near at that, since it took for granted the institutions of government, and, in true English style, concerned itself with

OVERLEAF: *winds off the Thames fan the flames of the Great Fire that raged for five days in 1666 and razed most of London.*

 such immediate issues as the unpopular actions of James II and forbade them in future. The settlement of 1689 showed how easy a settlement can be when people want it to be. The real secret of what has been called the Sensible Revolution (although for long enough it was called the Glorious Revolution, mainly because it was bloodless) is that England had a body of aristocrats who had everything to lose, principally their heads and their property, if they failed, and thenceforward the English got into the habit of thinking that all revolutions ought to be like their Revolution of 1688. Especially did they think this when, a century later, the French had a markedly different one, and even more so when after another century the Russians departed still further from the English model. "A small and temporary deviation," said Burke of the Revolution of 1688, or "a revolution not made but prevented," by which he meant that it was James II who had been trying to upset things, and the English Revolution had prevented things from being upset. The Revolution finally decided that the balance of power between king and parliament would be tipped in favor of the latter, giving England an executive who would function in concert with a sovereign legislative body. This was not determined at once, of course—it required years for the system to evolve, through development of a cabinet and the office of prime minister; but from 1689 onward, no king of England ever tried again to rule against the wishes, or in defiance, of parliament. All that remained to be done at the time was to provide for the succession after King William. This was accomplished by the Act of Settlement in 1701, stipulating that William should be followed by Princess Anne, daughter of the exiled James II by his first, and Protestant, wife. In the event of Anne's death without heirs, the crown was to go to Sophia, the electress of Hanover, the Protestant granddaughter of James I, and her heirs—a condition that reflected the determination of the squirearchy and the Anglican Church that the country should never again be ruled by a Roman Catholic king. When Anne and Sophia both died in 1714, George I came to the throne, and the house of Hanover was established after the troubled and troublesome house of Stuart. Under that house the country is still governed.

More important than any statute for the world in general was a book of the time. John Locke had written his second *Treatise on Government* before the Revolution of 1688, but it became its post-factum bible. It

*A 1698 oil portrait of William of Orange by Adriaen Key*

adumbrated two simple principles: that men set up government to preserve their property (which includes their lives), and that they may change it if and when it fails to do so. Locke did not think that men changed their government lightly, and he was quite sure that we must distinguish between the dissolution of government and the dissolution of society. All through his *Treatise* Locke is plainly writing about England and England's experience, and often he says so. "People are not so easily got out of their old forms [of government] as some are apt to suggest. . . . This slowness and aversion in the people to quit their old constitutions has in the many revolutions that have been seen in this kingdom, in this and former ages, still kept us to, or after some interval of fruitless attempts, still brought us back again to our old legislative of king, lords, and commons; and whatever provocations have made the crown be taken from some of our princes' heads, they never carried the people so far as to place it in another line." In other words, what Burke was to call a "small and temporary deviation" was a correct description of what happened in 1688. It was not really a revolution as 1789 or 1917 were revolutions. It was a dissolution of government and not in the least a dissolution of society.

The establishment of "Dutch William" and his wife in 1688–89, followed in due course by the Hanoverians in 1714, ensured England's future as a successful state and a world power. It put the country firmly on the side of the Protestant Dutch, and equally firmly in opposition to Catholic France. The alignment with the Dutch and against the French was what the exclusion of the later Stuarts (after Queen Anne) was all about. Not that much love was lost between England and Holland. Twice in the reign of Charles II they went to war as bitter commercial rivals; what brought them together after all was their common fear of the overmighty French king, Louis XIV, whose ambitions threatened the liberties, the religion, and the trade of the whole of western Europe. That was why Dutch William came to England, to build up a great alliance against the common enemy. King William fought against King Louis with tireless energy, if not with great success, at the head of allied forces by land and sea for many years, and he left the struggle as a legacy to his successor, Queen Anne, and her generalissimo, John Churchill, duke of Marlborough. Out of Marlborough's long contest with Louis came not simply a galaxy of great victories, from Blenheim

*Chinese lacquer cabinets were stylish in the late 1600s.*

to Malplaquet, but the Treaty of Utrecht, which gave his country the bases of England's first empire beyond the seas. No victory in the long history of European conflict was more decisive than Marlborough's at Blenheim in 1704—a triumph that broke the power of France for generations to come. As military strategist, tactician, war statesman, and diplomatist, Marlborough was second to none, and under this great captain was developed a new weapon which was to dominate land warfare for long years into the future. The infantry private, carrying a firearm topped with a bayonet, came into his own when he and his fellows were arrayed in a formation three lines deep, from which they could concentrate the maximum volume of fire power against an enemy. Although infantry maneuver in Marlborough's day was still in

*Blenheim Palace, Oxfordshire, the expansive countryseat created for the duke of Marlborough by the architects Vanbrugh and Hawksmoor*

its infancy, the techniques employed then were to lead to the tactics of Frederick the Great and Wellington. Yet more than military genius alone was responsible for Blenheim and the other victories: underlying them was Marlborough's extraordinary gift for combining land and sea power successfully in waging a world war that was backed by the growing financial, commercial, and maritime strength of England. The age to which Queen Anne gave her name was one in which the glory of the monarch owed almost everything to the glory of the society over which she reigned. In addition to Marlborough, the small nation of five and a half million people could boast of Wren, Newton, Pope, Addison, and Swift. It was a nation which, for all its political infighting, was united under one law and one parliament, and in possession of a sea power that would lead it to the ends of the earth. The terms of the Treaty of Utrecht in 1713 were to underwrite Great Britain's claim to great power rank, which would increase in eminence over the course of the next two centuries. In fact, the very title Great Britain was inaugurated by the war, which speeded formation of the union with Scotland and saw the founding of the British parliament in 1707.

The financial exigencies of the wars gave rise to both the national debt and the Bank of England. National finance had long been the private finance of the king or queen. In the reign of Queen Elizabeth I, England was still sometimes referred to as the Manor of England, as if it were the personal and private estate of the monarch. The king or queen was still expected, as in medieval times, to "live of his own," which literally meant *on* his own. Parliamentary grants were regarded as exceptional means of meeting exceptional occasions. In the reign of Queen Elizabeth, the ordinary revenue amounted to a good deal less than half a million pounds a year. It came from feudal income and rents (the Crown being still the biggest landowner in the country) and from such windfalls as the royal share of the plunder captured by sea dogs like Drake, which amounted to profits from piracy. The queen sometimes had subsidies from parliament, but these were occasional and unpopular. The English in these days, Bacon said, were "the least bitten in purse of any nation in Europe." Little wonder that wealthy subjects were in a position to build the magnificent houses for which Elizabethan England was famous. Lesser men paid hardly any taxes, nor was much that they consumed subject to customs and excise.

In the later seventeenth century, when wars at home and abroad were so expensive, government was on the lookout for new ways and means of raising money. One device resorted to was "a foreign tax with a foreign name," the excise, or *accise* (French) or *excijs* (Dutch), a particularly hateful impost because it was levied on home-produced articles of consumption instead of on the foreigner and his importations. As early as 1643 excise duty was put on ale, beer, cider, and perry (a fermented beverage made from pears), and two years later on salt, butcher's meat, hats, starch, copper, and various other commodities. It was in fact very like the taxation which aroused the American colonists a century later. So unpopular did it prove that various excise duties were always being removed, and other expedients like the hearth tax or the window tax resorted to. These again, involving the employment of "chimneymen" to count the number of hearths or windows in a citizen's house, often led to rioting, and (in the case of the hearth tax) had to be dropped, though the window tax survived until 1851. The exciseman, like the "preventive man" (who was supposed to guard the coastline against smuggling), was the favorite bogey of the popular imagination until long into the eighteenth century, when smuggling became a national industry, especially in Scotland.

Governments had recourse to long-term loans, of course, and an increasingly important class of moneyed men was engaged in negotiating, or underwriting, such loans. One such group founded the Bank of England, a private concern which went into business with the government, enjoying financial privileges in return for public service. Receiving a charter in 1694, the group had a capital of £1,200,000, and contracted to lend an equal sum to the government at 8 per cent interest. In return for this service the Bank received the monopoly of joint-stock banking in London, which was what its founders chiefly prized. This private bank became, it might be said, part of the constitution, and so did the national debt which it funded. If anything were to go wrong with the settlement of 1688–89, and particularly with the Protestant succession, the creditors of both the debt and the Bank would face ruin. The stability of both went together. So long as the Bank stood and the people with money in the fund, or invested in government securities, could be sure of their interest, the most influential people would have a stake in keeping the framework of church and state intact. By the same token, the exiled Stuarts and their Jacobite followers had no chance of success. Outside the pages of romantic fiction Jacobitism became increasingly illusory. The interconnection of England's financial and constitutional stability resembles closely Alexander Hamilton's planting of the American Constitution deep in the pockets of Federal stockholders. Nor were later Radicals like William Cobbett and Percy Bysshe Shelley, with their lurid language about "fundlords," the only critics of this regime of moneyed politics. Gladstone himself was fond of harping on the immorality of saddling posterity with our debts; it was, he said, a way of circumventing the benign dispensation of Providence in making war expensive.

There can be no more appropriate key word for English history after

*Sir Robert Walpole, statesman and public servant, is portrayed here by John Wootton as Master of the King's Staghounds in Windsor Forest.*

1694 than *finance*. It was no accident that the first great English novelist, even the founder of the novel, wrote *Robinson Crusoe* in 1719 as a parable of Economic Man pitting his lonely strength successfully against Nature. Among Daniel Defoe's best-known works on economics were *Public Credit* and *On Loans,* followed by his *General History of Trade*. Even less fortuitous is the fact that the man who became known as the first prime minister, Robert Walpole, was—as first lord of the Treasury—the first of a long line of financial wizards to hold the premiership. Not until comparatively recent times has the office of prime minister been officially recognized, with a salary attached. Only in the same tract of time, from Walpole to the present, has the lower house of parliament, or the House of Commons, become the predominant partner in the bicameral legislature. Whoever enjoyed primacy in paying the taxes (if the verb is not too ironical), for several centuries it has been the "lower" House, or the Commons, in whose name they were, and are, primarily levied. "The Commons, with the advice and consent of the Lords," is the formal phrase employed in financial legislation, on the assumption perhaps that he who pays the piper calls the tune.

Not only was the House of Commons to become the predominant house of parliament, but the Whig Party was to become the predominant party in the House of Commons. The two parties, Whigs and Tories, came by their names in the reign of Charles II—to be precise, during the Exclusion Bill crisis of 1680, when the king was trying to prevent the passing of a bill to exclude his brother, James, duke of York (the future James II) from succeeding to the throne. The objection to James was almost entirely on account of his adherence to the Roman Catholic religion; he had already resigned his post of lord high admiral, or commander-in-chief of the navy, after passage of the Test Act in 1673, which required all officeholders to accept (in effect) the sacramental rites of the Anglican Church. Charles II did his best to prevent the passing of an Exclusion Bill by not summoning parliament. Those who were anxious that parliament should meet petitioned the king to summon it, and were known as Petitioners, while those who abhorred any attempt to force the king to do so were called Abhorrers. The Petitioners were soon called Whigs and the Abhorrers, Tories, both names being slang terms of Irish origin and having no political content whatever. For the next two centuries, however, they were to remain the names of the two leading English parties. They do not signify in any straightforward way "progressive" and "conservative," let alone the "left" and "right" of latter-day parlance. To suppose that their differences can be expressed in terms of economic interests, of land and trade, would be far too great a simplification of their apposition. As in all else in those times religious differences were more important than political, and the Tories were on the whole Anglicans, whereas the Whigs generally sympathized with religious dissent.

William III tried to govern above party, but Queen Anne was a devout Anglican and showed a distinct partiality to the Tories; as a result they had the best of things until they lost ground when certain party members were suspected of planning a return of the exiled Stuarts upon the death of Queen Anne. The protagonist of the pro-Stuart Tories was Henry St. John, Viscount Bolingbroke, a brilliant but unreliable politician who made the mistake of hitching the wagon of his political fortunes to the waning star of the exiled family. When Queen Anne died, the Protestant successor to the throne, George Louis, elector of Hanover, arrived and took charge before Bolingbroke and his section of the Tories could step in, and not only was Bolingbroke compelled to spend much of the remainder of his life in political exile, but the Tory Party as a whole was tainted with the suspicion of treason. For many years the Tories, though numerous, were not, as the saying goes, of sound ministerial timber. Strictly speaking, the Tory Party remained out of office as a party until the birth of a new Toryism was brought into being nearly a century later by the Younger Pitt. Historians have learned however, that party names meant very little during the eighteenth century: the Tories may have been out of office, but men of Tory sentiment were more numerous than any other kind of men in the country. As Dr. Johnson, the great despiser of Whigs, liked to say: if the country were fairly polled, the Hanoverians and their followers would be out of office tonight, and packed out of the country by tomorrow morning. The fact was, however, that the Whigs were to all intents and purposes England, and England was the Whigs. They were the party of the present, of peace, prosperity, and progress. Perhaps, on the whole, it would be best to say that they stood for success.

So England had come through her revolutionary century, after a

*Periwigged patrons of a coffeehouse smoke, debate, and drink the murky brew.*

*This pro-Tory propaganda piece depicts Daniel Defoe as devil and pope.*

civil war of pulled punches, and a great deal of skillful maneuvering to avoid a repetition thereof, with a stable dynasty ("as safe as the Bank of England," men said) and a national debt that kept a very large propertied class loyal to established institutions in church and state. By the end of Queen Anne's reign England had won, largely by the genius of "the old corporal," John Churchill, a splendid reputation for success in arms. The eighteenth century was to be, if not her finest hour, her most successful, and as she embarked upon the Hanoverian age, Britain entered one of the most glowing periods of her modern history. The countryside was a vista of stepped roofs and Dutch gardens, Palladian facades and ornamental waters, neatly hedged fields and fat sheep, with quiet market towns in the middle distance and dense woodland closing the horizon. Civil life had become civilian, urban life more urbane (there were in London by the year 1708 some three thousand coffeehouses—those small centers of urbanity). The country house was little more than a town house set down in the countryside, and by the early years of the eighteenth century the squire was doing his best to compete with the townsman in equipping his dwelling with sash windows and wainscot, ceilings of plaster, and fireplaces of marble. The dawning age, over whose destiny those country squires would hold such sway, was to see the founding of the first British Empire, the loss of America, the first critical experience of financial speculation, and the beginnings of modern industry and agriculture. 

CHAPTER VII

# ENGLAND IN THE AGE OF REVOLUTIONS

England, as has been noted, became Great Britain some years before the end of the war with Louis XIV and the peace of Utrecht in 1713. It was not simply a matter of territorial accessions or military prestige. The adoption of "Great Britain" as an official title came in the middle of the war, three years after the Battle of Blenheim and two years after the Battle of Ramillies, in consequence of the Act of Union between England and Scotland in 1707. There had been a dynastic union after 1603 when James VI of Scotland became James I of England, but in 1707 the two kingdoms became one, under the name of Great Britain, with a single parliament at Westminster. The Scots were to be represented by forty-five members in the House of Commons and sixteen peers in the House of Lords. They were exempted from the war taxes and retained their own (Presbyterian) church, and their own Scots law and judicial procedure, but they adopted English weights and coinage. All commercial restrictions were removed between the two countries, and the Union Jack, which embodied the cross of Saint Andrew with that of Saint George (the patron saints of the respective countries), was adopted as a common flag.

*Chiswick, Lord Burlington's Palladian-style villa outside London*

The Scots complained a good deal of the unequal nature of the partnership between two peoples of such disparate wealth. On the other hand, Englishmen have generally been ready to admit without undue rancor that 1707 merely marks one more conquest of England by the Scots. From that date the Scots were to take a large share in running the British Empire overseas and in staffing the British army; they were to contribute some of the finest front-line regiments to the forces of the Crown, and it is said that wherever there is a trading station which hoists the Union Jack or a steamship which wears the Red Ensign you will find a man whose name begins with "Mac" in effective command.

When the war with Louis XIV came to an end, Great Britain also came to terms with France's ally, the Spanish monarchy. France ceded to Great Britain such valuable outposts of empire as Newfoundland, Nova Scotia, Hudson Bay and Strait, together with the island of Saint Christopher in the West Indies. Spain ceded to her the Rock of Gibraltar which she had lost early in the war, and the flanking island of Minorca. Thus in part at least, as biblical fundamentalists like to recite, the promise came true that England should "possess the gates of her enemies." She also handed over to her a share of the trade in Negro slaves with North America. Along with certain territories which came to her during the next half century or more, Britain was acquiring the key points of the dominions which were to comprise the British Empire. And at the end of the war, typically, she discarded the man who had served her most brilliantly in arms. John Churchill, duke of Marlborough, frequently behaved like a scoundrel, but his country's treatment of him after the most dazzling succession of victories that a general ever offered his sovereign is in retrospect only more ungrateful than that meted out to another Churchill who rode the whirlwind and controlled the storm in a later century. After that, political affairs were to be pre-empted for many years by what was called the Robinocracy, or the followers of Sir Robert Walpole. After becoming first lord of the Treasury and chancellor of the Exchequer, Walpole demonstrated not only his talents in the realm of finance but also his wizardry in political maneuver—so much so that he is rightly known as the first prime minister. For more than twenty years he held the essential position under a monarchical constitution: that is, he held the House of Commons because he possessed the royal favor, and he was indispensable to the king because he alone could manage the Commons. Despite their inability to speak English, George I and George II were masters of their own affairs in everything that counted with them, and Walpole knew it. It was his genius to persuade the monarch that he wanted what Walpole wanted. "Pudding-time" these years were termed by that cheerful timeserver, the vicar of Bray, who was always to be found on the right side, whatever king might reign. The relevant verse of his song is:

*When George and Pudding-time came o'er,*
*And moderate men looked big, sir,*
*I turned a cat-in-the-pan once more,*
*And so became a Whig, sir.*

The Hanoverian sovereigns themselves had to be Whigs, too, or at least put their trust in Whigs since there was no one else they could put their trust in. For the greater part of the eighteenth century there were enough varieties of the species to suit everyone's tastes or interests, *pace* Dr. Johnson. By the time Walpole resigned in 1742, there was no question of Whigs giving way to the Tories. The great Tory Party of the age of Queen Anne had gone to pieces on the shoals of Jacobitism, and Robinocracy had made England safe for Whiggery for another fifty years. The laws and customs of Walpole's time were made to order for the squires and the Anglican clergy, who perceived that continuance of the house of Hanover meant security and maintenance of the status quo. Theirs was a world in which political power was based upon influence—influence perpetuated through the dispensation of crown patronage, through sinecures, pensions, jobs for dependents, and commissions or church livings for younger sons.

Politics at this time had ceased to be ideological, if they had ever been so. Even the Jacobites, clinging to a romantic vision of the exiled Stuarts, and prepared to draw the sword (but not enough swords) in two rebellions, in 1715 and 1745, seem scarcely to have believed in, or only half wished for, their return. The attempt of James, exiled son of the deposed James II, to reclaim the throne in 1715 came to nothing. In 1745, under his son Charles Stuart—Bonnie Prince Charlie—rebellious troops marching out of Scotland reached Derby, within a hundred miles of London. At that point people were selling government securities like wagers at a horse race. But in 1746 those rebels were cruelly slaughtered at Culloden Moor and the survivors dispersed. The last squalid days of the prince in exile formed a wretched epilogue to the high adventure that had carried him so close to his goal. A pitched battle on English soil had become unimaginable. Bulls and bears charmed the English greatly more than swords would ever do again.

With Walpole and the Whigs England had, once and for all, turned civilian. She fought many wars, but they were a long way off, and the contestants were regular soldiers fighting for pay. They seem to have felt about the sword in those days as Dr. Johnson said he thought about the pen when he declared that no man but a blockhead ever wrote except for money. It may well have been true, as Burke would claim, that the age of chivalry was dead. It was certainly true that the age of economists and calculators had come. Whether it was Napoleon or Adam Smith who called the English a nation of shopkeepers, it was someone speaking in the eighteenth century, which was the age of Jeremy Bentham and his gospel of utility. When he wrote his *Fragment on Government* in 1776 that economist and philosopher begged his readers not to blame him if he wrote, and spoke, "a mercenary language," for, he asked, if we are not to say that happiness or pleasure can be measured in terms of money, is there anything meaningful that the legislator can say about it? Quantity, not quality, alone is measurable, and law and the legislator can be, and should be, interested in nothing else.

This is one of the things that repelled, and continues to repel, many people about eighteenth-century England. "Soul dead, stomach well-alive" was how Thomas Carlyle was to summarize it, and there undoubtedly was a certain coarseness of fiber about a century that began with Walpole's port and partridges and ended with Bentham's "Felicific Calculus." Walpole's latest and greatest biographer has shown us that the great Whig statesman was interested in and knowledgeable about even more ancient and noble things than game birds and wine: the splendid pictures he bought for his collection at Houghton Hall are evidence of that. Nor was the "pig-philosophy," as Thomas Carlyle nicknamed the teaching of Jeremy Bentham, with its calculus of pleasures and pains, the whole of utilitarianism.

It certainly was in that age that public houses could advertise un-

*William Hogarth's "Gin Lane" illustrates the pitfalls of intemperance.*

ashamedly "Drunk for a penny, dead-drunk for tuppence, clean straw to lie on for nothing." The very island which was said to "have arisen at Heaven's command from out the azure main" seemed to be floating to shipwreck on a sea of gin and had to be rescued from race suicide by measures like the Gin Act of 1736 which only put the brake on by making the poison too expensive. The national passion for gambling reached the point where men would hazard fortunes on a race between two flies across the bald pate of a parson. Nor were these activities the prerogative of the "rich and profligate," terms which were coupled in that time like "poor but honest." They did not wait upon the dawn of the permissive society. The London of Hogarth, the England of Smollett, were familiar with a brutality and a beastliness that would put the choicest efforts of the twentieth century itself to shame.

Actually they put the eighteenth century to shame, for this age of crapulous levity was also the age of the revivalists Wesley and White-

*Jacobite prisoners guarded by their Loyalist captors after vainly attempting to restore the Stuarts to the throne* field, or reformers like John Howard and Robert Raikes and the movement for "ragged schools," of the mysticism of William Law's "Serious Call to a Devout and Holy Life" (which had much influence upon Samuel Johnson's religious thinking), and of Thomas Clarkson and the antislavery movement. The fact is that England wore her eighteenth century with a difference. Instead of the brittle rationalism we associate with the Age of Reason, England was entering into the age of feeling, of sentiment if not of sentimentality, of humanitarianism, of philanthropy, and of religious revival. The portrait of Jeremy Bentham reveals a handsome brother of Mr. Pickwick rather than an iron-jawed grinder of the faces of the poor, or personification of heartlessness. Bentham fought all his long life for the cause of human happiness, for the balance of pleasure over pain. King George III himself lived an exemplary family life and believed himself to be fighting for the cause of virtue and religion in a world of dirty politicians every bit as heroically as Saint George fought the dragon, and twice as self-righteously.

The heartless calm of the eighteenth century is a myth, largely invented by writers who were not happy in it, like Jean Jacques Rousseau, who could not indeed have been happy at any time or in any country in history, in fact who refused to believe that men were put on earth to be happy. The venom that Rousseau, and some others like him, squirted into the face of their age still lingers around its memory. Fortunately the age was heading for revolution, American, French, Industrial. Had it staked its claim to immortality on its celebrated sweetness of life, the smile of reason would have faded into a grin of fatuous self-satisfaction like the grin of the Cheshire cat.

Europe was on the way to a new religion, the religion of humanity, whose gods—or idols—were called English, but it was native to no special soil. France was to be the first country conquered by it, through the enlargement of the French Revolution, and it conquered as a religion conquers. This was perhaps hardly grasped until 1856 when Alexis de Tocqueville wrote his great book, *L'Ancien Régime et la révolution.* In the third chapter of that illuminating work, he says: "No previous political upheaval, however violent, had aroused such passionate enthusiasm, for the ideal the French Revolution set before it was not merely a change in the French social system but nothing short of a regeneration of the whole human race. . . . It would be truer to say that it developed into a species of religion, if a singularly imperfect one, since it was without a God, without a ritual or promise of a future life. Nevertheless, this strange religion has, like Islam, overrun the whole world. . . ."

England, true to her idiosyncratic way of historical development, experienced this revolutionary contagion in a way all her own. This was in part at least because she had had revolutions (in a limited sense) before, and not least because she had a revolution in her dominion in North America. It would perhaps be misleading to say that she had received inoculation. Few things about the French Revolution, however, are more strange than the singular coolness with which it was received in England. It had its enthusiasts, of course, but the country rallied with wonderful unanimity to defend the national mores against it.

An Englishman finds it hard to believe that England was already the land of revolutions, so untroubled does the surface of life appear for long periods. "Pudding-time" is hardly the epithet for a revolutionary epoch. The illusion was in part due to the legerdemain of Sir Robert Walpole with his famous cult of *quieta non movere,* or letting sleeping dogs lie. For twenty-one years, from 1721 to 1742, this Norfolk squire seems to sit at the head of England like a drayman seated on the head of a prostrate horse. He boasted to Queen Caroline in 1734, during the War of the Polish Succession, "Madam, there are fifty thousand men slain this year in Europe, and not one Englishman." He might have said—indeed he did say—that England's chief interest was peace. She had given hostages to fortune in exiling the house of Stuart, and for a long time the Stuart cause was that of England's enemies, but the fact that none of them ventured to espouse it at all vigorously was in large part due to Walpole's skill and industry in the field of foreign relations.

The sheet anchor of Walpole's foreign policy was friendship with France, whose new king, the youthful Louis XV, was scarcely more safely enthroned in France than was George I in England, so that the two old enemies shared a common interest, which kept them in alliance for a record period of time. In Cardinal Fleury, France had a statesman who was in most respects Walpole's opposite number, and the strange conjunction of squire and cardinal kept the peace of Europe

*John Wesley led a religious revival and founded the Methodist Church.*

 more or less intact for some seventeen years. Not that there were no wars, for by the First Family Compact of 1733 France had also as an ally England's old enemy, Spain, a Spain concerned to recover Gibraltar and to preserve her monopoly of trade on the Spanish Main from the incursions of English poachers. Open war with Spain came in 1739, a war that was to be known as the War of Jenkins' Ear, after the supposed mutilation of a British sea captain by Spanish coast guards. Brought before the House of Commons, he produced his ear in a bottle, and in response to the question of what he had done, the captain replied, "I commended my soul to God and my cause to my country." It was just the sort of slogan to appeal to the public imagination, and for the cause of Jenkins' ear, England went to war.

Nobody much wanted to fight, except the London mobs and Walpole's political enemies who saw in it the likelihood of his failing to pursue it successfully and thereby losing office. Indeed the Spaniards had met England's demands quite amiably before the war began. Along with the Crimean War little more than a century later, the War of Jenkins' Ear remains the classic case of a war forced on the government by the people, or at any rate by a noisy section of it. It also provides a vivid illustration of the factious politics of eighteenth-century England. The truth was that after more than a decade and a half of it, England was tired of peace, and any excuse was good enough for a fight. Indeed, the war with Spain led into the greater European War of the Austrian Succession, and thereafter into the first world war of modern history, all within a quarter of a century that ended with England mistress of Canada and India. As so often happens, little wars lead to big ones, and in the course of the story England passed from the leadership of her greatest peace minister in the person of Robert Walpole to that of her greatest war minister in that of William Pitt, earl of Chatham. At the time Pitt first joined the ministry as secretary of state in 1756 Frederick the Great declared, "England has long been in labor, but at last she has brought forth a man."

Pitt had every quality that Walpole lacked. If Walpole stands for England the great shopkeeper rising to fortune on a heap of soap and candles, tea and sugar, Pitt stands for England rising to the height of an imperial destiny. He would not tolerate any sniggering at the "piddling tricks of trade" in his presence. He nursed a vision of his country's imperial greatness, and he could utter it in words. Few of his speeches have come down to us, but many who listened to them have vouched for their magnificence. Men caught greatness from that wonderful voice. A monumental inscription in London speaks of "a certain kind of happy contagion of his probity and spirit" which brought about the augmentation of the Empire and the restoration of the ancient reputation and influence of his country.

People bequeathed fortunes to the great patriot (as the citizens of old Rome were wont to do when they wished not so much to reward, as to testify to the greatness of their leaders). Sarah, duchess of Marlborough, was one such benefactor; a Somerset gentleman left him an estate at Burton Pynsent; the people of New York put up a white marble statue of him in Wall Street; in the Pump Room at Bath they stood up while he drank his glass of water. Such was the genius of the Pitts, father and son, that people took it for granted that nothing much could go wrong while one or other of them was at the head of affairs. "I know that I can save this country, and that no one else can," said the Great Commoner, and they believed him, because he did. Wolfe in Canada, Clive in India, served as his lieutenants, but it was William Pitt who pulled the strings, and everyone knew it and applauded it, except such insectivorous observers as George III. By giving back to politics a soul, something that had been lacking since the days of Cromwell, the Elder Pitt served his country well, for it is not only in war that, according to Napoleon's reckoning, the moral is to the physical as three is to one.

Pitt was an eccentric genius who resigned in 1761 because his colleagues refused to go to war with France's ally, Spain. The war over which he had presided, which was the first truly global conflict, yielded the riches of world trade and the command of overseas trade routes, but it had put a heavy strain on Britain's resources. In 1763 British authority over Canada, India, and parts of the West Indies was recognized by the Treaty of Paris, ending the Seven Years' War, and the nation obtained a foothold in Africa and the western Mediterranean; but a trade recession threatened, and even Pitt's friends in the financial community felt it was time to pause to digest the fruits of victory. With Pitt gone (to endure temporary eclipse as the earl of Chatham), it seemed to many that the glorious times had departed with him, and

*Benjamin West's romanticized portrayal of James Wolfe, who was mortally wounded on the field while routing the French at Quebec*

their suspicions were proved correct in the next two decades, which witnessed the visionless politics of little men that culminated in the loss of the empire in the New World which Pitt had done so much to attain. He was to die on his crutches, storming in the House of Lords against George III and Lord North's disastrous policies in the colonies.

The young man who became King George III in 1760 knew full well that he could never be king of England while Pitt ruled in the hearts of his people, and the irony of it was that no man in England shared the patriotic moralism of George III so much as William Pitt. The king was eager to play his required role in the delicately balanced constitutional monarchy, a role demanding that the monarch be the "governor" of the machine. But at a time when the balance between executive and legislative was swinging toward parliamentary control, the throne was occupied by a neurotically self-mistrustful man, suspicious of politicians in general, pathetically drawn to nonentities like the earl of Bute, who became his chief minister. For years to come the king's governments would be coalitions, Whiggish in character, formed and re-formed while he sought to find a man who would serve him faithfully against the machinations of politicians.

What Horace Walpole called "the private and lifeless solitude" of the king's youth had isolated George III from the world of the men with whom he would have to function as king. He came to see himself as an agent sent by God to redeem his country from the vicious and the clever; preferring morals over mind, and persons over ideas, his was the tragedy of good intentions stupidly executed. Conscientious to a fault, he had an infinite capacity for details, and very little for mastering the larger issues. A man of unusual moral courage, he was both obstinate and blunt, and his stubbornness was an important factor in stiffening the resolve of his ministers. "It is with the utmost astonishment that I find any of my subjects capable of encouraging the rebellious disposition which unhappily exists in some of my colonies in America," he said. "Having entire confidence in the wisdom of my Parliament, the Great Council of the Nation, I will steadily pursue those measures which they have recommended for the support of the constitutional rights of Great Britain and the protection of the commercial interests of my kingdom." Slowly and sadly he learned that the dirty arts of the politics he detested were indispensable to the system over which he reigned, and that no one could govern without them. Soon after George Grenville succeeded Lord Bute in 1763, the first sounds of revolution beyond the seas could be heard. Grenville's Stamp Act, passed by parliament in the belief that the American colonists should help foot the bill for the war that had removed the French threat from North America, appealed greatly to country gentlemen who were paying a land tax of 4 shillings on the pound and who considered themselves the most highly taxed people in the world. This was only one of many measures by which the government proposed to increase revenue from America, and most of them were aimed at reducing smuggling and the cost of collecting duties. The difficulty was that all these programs were in such marked contrast to the years of salutary neglect the colonies had enjoyed during the time of Walpole and earlier, and they had the effect of aggravating the most lively, vocal elements in colonial society—attorneys, journalists, and shopkeepers who had an important voice in the molding of public opinion.

Neither at this time nor earlier had the Americans suffered any real oppression from British rule. At the root of their opposition to the policies of George III's ministers was the subjugation of their interests to those of English merchants trading in the New World—a corollary of the old system by which the monopoly of colonial trade in the interests of British merchants and manufacturers was held to be the principal reason for empire. As matters developed, the Americans were not simply opposed to the Stamp Act or to other impositions of taxation without representation; they were refusing to be taxed by anyone except themselves. (After the Rockingham government, in the face of colonial outcries, repealed the Stamp Act in 1766, it coupled repeal with a Declaratory Act which reasserted the right of parliament to tax the colonists.) Americans were also revealing a consciousness of what a later generation would call Manifest Destiny in their resistance to the royal proclamation prohibiting further westward expansion. From beginning to end, the American Revolution was the work of an active minority, a native governing class of merchants and landowners whose interests were threatened by imperial policies and by the barrier to obtaining western land, and who undertook to correct such matters.

The king was particularly unfortunate in his choice of ministers throughout the deepening conflict. Grenville was an excellent man of

business, but he lacked flexibility and was a bore. ("When he has wearied me for two hours," George III complained, "he looks at his watch to see if he may not tire me for one hour more.") When he could stand Grenville no longer, the king turned to Chatham, was refused, and settled for Rockingham's Whigs, who lasted only twelve months in office. Then Chatham accepted the task, fell ill, and was replaced by the duke of Grafton, whose chancellor of the Exchequer, Charles Townshend, angered the colonists further with his policies and provoked the Boston Tea Party. Finally the king found what he thought was salva-

*A British cartoonist's allegorical depiction of the Teapot Tempest*
OVERLEAF: *the British ship* Serapis *and the* Bonhomme Richard, *1779*

tion in the person of Frederick, Lord North, a sweet-tempered man who was fatally unwilling to disoblige his sovereign, and to whom he clung for twelve years until the colonies were lost beyond recall. Subduing the rebellious Americans was never to be an easy proposition, given the immense distance and the logistics involved, but it was even less likely because North was no Pitt, and the British general staff a far cry from the likes of Clive and Wolfe. Worst of all, the Colonial Office fell into the hands of Lord George Germain, a soldier declared incompetent and unworthy to serve His Majesty after the Battle of Minden in 1759, whose failure to give proper instructions to General William Howe was a significant factor in the surrender of seven thousand troops to the Americans at Saratoga in 1777. After Saratoga the French entered the war on the side of the rebels; the next year Spain joined the anti-British coalition; Holland followed in 1780; and in 1781 Prussia and Austria were leagued with the Baltic powers in opposition to Britain. The country, it seemed, was without a friend in the world, and by 1779 the British Isles were in imminent danger of invasion by the French and Spanish. Admiral Rodney defeated the Spanish fleet off Cape Saint Vincent in 1780, but within a year the French under De Grasse were in the Chesapeake, making inevitable the British surrender at Yorktown. When news of that defeat reached England, Lord North paced his room, exclaiming, "Thank God, it is all over!" The opposition closed ranks in the Commons, riotous meetings were held in London, and the following March North submitted his resignation. "At last the fatal day has come," said the king, who even talked of abdication. Yet the war was not over; there were to be naval victories by Rodney, and the siege of Gibraltar was lifted after a magnificent defense lasting three years, and these feats gave Britain a better bargaining position when peace finally came. At the end of 1782 Great Britain acknowledged the independence of the United States of America. The young William Pitt, who served as chancellor of the Exchequer in Lord Shelburne's ministry and was leader of the House of Commons at the age of twenty-four, negotiated a treaty of peace with a world of enemies.

After the final defeat at Yorktown, Englishmen were under no delusion about what had happened. The French navy, not the American farmers, had beaten them, and when they saw the torch of liberty car-

*William Pitt (the Elder), charismatic advocate of British expansion*

ried to the shores of France in 1789 they watched with a sense that retribution was being made. The loss of the colonies might have been expected to provide Britain with a salutary lesson in governing dependent peoples. Certainly there were men who, during the course of the conflict, had warned their countrymen of the attendant risks, and who had applauded the rebels as fighting the old battle of all Englishmen who believed in freedom. "We cannot, I fear, falsify the pedigree of this fierce people," Burke said during the war, "and persuade them that they are not sprung from a nation in whose veins the blood of freedom

*A British cartoon of 1780 makes light of America and her European allies, and shows the scales still tipped in England's favor.*

circulates." To Burke the issue was one of humanity, morality, and generosity—those virtues that begin where law ends. "The question with me is, not whether you have a right to make your people miserable," he argued, "but whether it is not your interest to make them happy."

"You have taught me to look elsewhere than to the Commons for the sense of my subjects," George III once said to William Pitt. There were numerous tribunes of the commoners, voices of popular feeling, in eighteenth-century England, and extremely few of them gave utterance within the walls of parliament, that preserve of landowners and moneyed men, great and small. Apart from Burke and Pitt, the Great Commoner, who seemed always to speak from a sphere above politics, and certainly above party, there was John Wilkes who in his running fight with both executive and legislative branches of government claimed to speak for the "middling and inferior set of people." There was John Wesley who, although he was an autocrat and a Tory in his politics, spent most of his life pushing open the doors of Heaven (and the gates of Hell) for the entry of the meanest of God's creatures. All these, and many more, represented a populism that was on the move in western Europe, and not least in England. What was happening in the world at this time goes largely unperceived, and certainly misunderstood, by all who keep their gaze fixed upon the facade of political institutions.

CHAPTER VIII

# THE FIRST INDUSTRIAL NATION

Writing of his boyhood, back in the "dark ages" of the eighteenth century, William Cobbett, the journalist and reformer, recalled that the country people of England never knew or thought much about politics in those days. Only occasionally, he said, "The shouts of victory or the murmur at a defeat would now-and-then break in upon our tranquillity for a moment." In fact, he could not remember ever having seen a newspaper in the house. Then, after the American war had continued for a time, "We became a little better acquainted with subjects of this kind." By the last third of the century, English society had grown more complex and more divided than ever before. The aristocracy was richer; wealthy Englishmen built private laboratories and libraries and follies, constructed elaborate gardens and spacious Georgian homes, adorned their houses with silver and porcelain and with the art treasures they had collected on grand tours of the Continent. At the other extreme of the economic scale life was cruel, hard, and frequently violent. The poor starved in vile slums and were herded into jails as the laws for petty crime became ever more harsh; there were epidemics of disease; rioting erupted in city and countryside, where

*Trafalgar Square, commemorating Admiral Nelson's famous naval triumph*

enormous wealth was an accompaniment to the worst poverty. After the defeat at the hands of American backwoodsmen and shopkeepers (and their French allies) there was a sense of national shame; yet there existed also a new and widespread belief that the future belonged somehow to Britain. One reason why the English were not troubled for long by the loss of their American colonies was their increasing preoccupation with an enormous event that was taking place at home.

Behind the facade of politics, removed from wars and rebellions, quietly, unobtrusively, with only the hushed breath of escaping steam or the low grunt of a steam-hammer beside a river, the greatest revolution in human history was getting under way. Of all the revolutions of this revolutionary age, the one called the Industrial Revolution was at

*"Rain, Steam, and Speed," J.M.W. Turner's poetic evocation of a train*

the same time the most stealthy in its approach and the most dramatic in its denouement. By its very nature it was the least likely to be announced until it arrived. Here and there, out of sight and for long out of mind—spots of a darker hue were spreading silently beneath the green vesture of the land in which it manifested itself, until one day men told each other that the world was changed—for the worst. At first many, including the artists, were full of admiration for it. The poetasters too were ready to celebrate man's technical achievements, and there is no better account of these things than the detailed descriptions by Erasmus Darwin in "The Loves of the Plants," from his work *Botanic Garden; The Temple of Nature.* It was many years before poets took to rural escapism, for the truth is that the first fruits of the industrial society were not as ugly as the urban landscapes of the next century. Train and factory flashed with flames and fire. They possessed many of the features of the sublime, so dear to the romantics.

Why was England the earliest scene of this revolution? In the first place she had the right kind of geography and geology: mineral deposits and strata of coal located in close proximity, and both within reasonable distance of the seaports. Then England was the nation of the Royal Society and the advance of science. In those branches of industry which were the backbone of industrial development—iron and steel and cotton manufacture—the ground was hardly at all cluttered up by medieval survivals like guilds, and the country was free of internal customs barriers. Patent law barely put any real restriction on the exchange, let alone the theft, of technical improvements. The orthodox political economy was that of free trade, or *laissez faire;* the banking system made capital plentiful; and Protestant dissent, especially by the Quakers, upheld high standards of financial probity.

This revolution had been long in the making, and there is no one date to which a beginning may be assigned. Nor did Englishmen of the time speak of an "industrial revolution"—not until later were they fully aware of the gigantic dimensions of what had taken place. While Pitt and Clive and Wolfe were founding the first British Empire, men like Richard Arkwright were quietly establishing the foundations of the great movement that was to make Britain the workshop of the world, and in the 1770s and 1780s these pioneers were regarded with admiration and wonder. When in 1759 James Brindley constructed an aqueduct forty feet high above the river to carry coal from the duke of Bridgewater's collieries to Manchester, he was regarded as a magician; after all, he had halved the cost of coal in Manchester and made possible the mechanization of the cotton industry in Lancashire. And a decade later, when Arkwright established his spinning mills at Cromford, he set in motion a complete factory system based upon power-driven machinery. Josiah Wedgwood revolutionized the pottery industry by his use of new materials, precision tools, assembly lines, and advertising, and he even promoted the construction of canals to speed his wares to the export market. In company with Arkwright, James Hargreaves and Samuel Crompton dramatically improved the production of textiles; John Wilkinson demonstrated what could be done with iron. As the agriculturist Arthur Young wrote, "A vast change has taken place in English social life within two generations. View the navigation, the roads, the harbours, and all other public works. Take notice of the spirit with which manufactures are carried on. . . . Move your eye which side you will, you behold nothing but great riches and yet greater resources." Many of the inventions that made the revolution possible had been made long before, but became operative late in the century for political and other reasons. England had (or thought she had) solved the problem of orderly government; manpower for the new mills was readily available because of an enormous increase in population; there were few restraints on enterprise in the form of regulation or control; and above all, there existed at the time an attitude of mind which was no less than a scientific outlook on the world. There was a communion between the men of science and the craftsmen, a shared conviction that by understanding nature man could control it, and a widespread desire to understand the technical achievements of the age. Midland towns bristled with intellectual life, scientific societies flourished, the spirit of inquiry dominated men's minds. Beginning with the reign of George III the first improvements in transportation were made since the days of Roman Britain: a network of canals reached out across the land, roads were macadamized, railways constructed. Even the ancient methods of agriculture underwent marked change: Robert Bakewell began raising woolier sheep and fatter cattle; "Turnip" Townshend adopted new techniques to increase the land's productivity and began writing crop rotation into the leases of his ten-

*Josiah Wedgwood, from a jasper-ware medallion produced at his pottery*

ant farmers. As men, women, and children poured into the new industrial centers and the coalpits to "bow their heads for bread," rural England became increasingly a land of large farms and enclosed fields, a breadbasket to support the growing urban population.

The wonder years of the rise of sustained economic growth were the central decades of George III's reign, when the British economy, and indeed society in general, were transformed in such a way that in the future economic expansion became more or less automatic. The economy moved from a lower to a higher state of production as the framework of a modern industrial system came into existence. The figures of industrial output tell only part of the story: coal production doubled, and the manufacture of pig iron and the import of raw cotton quadru-

*Newcomen engines, like the one pictured here, helped mechanize the production of coal in English mines in the early 1700s.*

pled. Overall, industrial output increased twofold between 1780 and 1800, a speed which was to be multiplied in the future. In 1814 Patrick Colquhoun published his *Treatise on the Wealth, Power and Resources of the British Empire,* and he was not exaggerating when he said that "an era had arrived in the affairs of the British Empire, discovering resources which have excited the wonder, the astonishment, and perhaps the envy of the civilized world."

Political stability and the solution of constitutional problems in the seventeenth century had left the national energies free to exercise themselves more vigorously in the spheres of trade and industry in the eighteenth. Most other forms of innovation could be, and were, postponed for long years in the "sleeping-dog" period of Walpole and the overseas expansion, east and west, presided over by Chatham. Civil war and revolution were left behind by the time England entered upon the energetic courses which carried through her Industrial Revolution. The use of that term is legitimate so long as we bear in mind that it was more than an industrial revolution, and that it marked a social transformation that gave birth to modern English society. As one English historian has said: "Most of what we recognize around us as contemporary, as most characteristic of the mid-twentieth century, not merely in the achievements of science and technology, but in social and political organization, is the direct, logistic development of forces set in motion in the Britain of George III." When he sought what his book calls "the English Inheritance," Dr. Kitson Clark concluded: "we inherit from the seventeenth century, from the Tudors, from medieval England, from the Romans, or Saxons or Ancient Britons if you will, but we inherit through the eighteenth century; the eighteenth and nineteenth centuries have left their marks on all the goods that come to us."

Those are the key words: "inherit *through*. . . ." Precisely what were the marks which the eighteenth and nineteenth centuries left on our goods? It is not a matter in which precision is possible, for it is largely a matter of style, and style is apt to be insusceptible to exact measurement or close description. The most and the best that can be said perhaps is that the eighteenth century left upon our "goods" the imprint of common sense, of utility, of reasonableness. It may be that the country was passing from mysticism to logic, or, in everyday terms, from humbug to humdrum. The transition often seemed to threaten a decline in gentleness, even in cultivation, yet as the darker aspects of an acquisitive society menaced the traditional values of an older civilization, society sought salvation in the traditional patterns of social morality. Evangelical Protestantism and the High Church movement which we associate with the name of Oxford, that is, the Oxford movement, proved to be the spiritual accompaniments of the first industrial society.

In sheer magnitude, the Industrial Revolution was perhaps diminutive when compared with the economic upheavals that have occurred since, but in comparison with anything that had happened up to that time in the Western world, it was gigantic, and has indeed been likened to the stealing of fire from Heaven and the kindling of it on earth by Prometheus. In many respects the revolution must have had the purgative effect which Aristotle associated with the pity and terror produced by great tragedy, although at the time neither pity nor terror were greatly in evidence. It has only been since those heroic days that British observers have found it painful to face the consequences of industrial development in terms of the human suffering it produced. It is almost impossible for us to comprehend the shock delivered to the human psyche by the creation of the industrial town, where none had existed before. There had never been anything like it in the history of the world, and in more recent years smoke-abatement laws and the replacement of coal-burning machinery by electricity have changed the whole aspect of industrial society. The poet Blake's "dark satanic mills" belong to only a comparatively short period of history. When the Nottingham poet Henry Kirke White wrote his celebrated poem "Clifton Grove" in 1803, the worst he could say of the industrial town where he was born was in a reference to the horizon:

*. . . where the town's blue turrets dimly rise*
*And manufacture taints the ambient skies . . .*

People were on the whole proud of the latest triumphs of industry, but they were often afraid, too. What had happened to the men and women who had vanished into the smoke? Once it had been possible to see them, almost to parade them, each week in the parish church. In the villages, Sundays had been a roll call under the watchful eye of squire and parson, from a high pew and pulpit. But in the industrial north and the Midlands such superintendence was now breaking down. For one thing, there were not enough churches, and for another, many workers were ceasing to attend them. Lord Liverpool, prime minister in some of the most anxious years of industrialization, spent a good deal of time over the Church Building Act of 1818. These new churches were designed as outposts in the battle against the dangerous and advancing forces of political democracy and religious dissent, yet it was this kind of thing—sincerely pious in intention, as well as a part of the strategy of social security—that gave rise to the Marxist gibe that religion was the opium of the people.

The darkest years of England's transition to the modern industrial society were those when she was confronted by revolution in both America and France. After the Seven Years' War when the English rule

*The subscription room at Lloyd's of London*

*The Bank of England in 1808*

replaced the French in Canada and India, many people at home and abroad foresaw the loss of the American colonies. Vergennes, who was the French foreign minister at the time, knew what he was saying when he prophesied that the English would "ere long repent the removal of the only check that kept their colonies in awe—that is, fear of the French presence." 

Not so many, perhaps, foresaw the spread of revolution from America to France, a process that was to be celebrated when the revolutionaries sent a key to the captured Bastille to President Washington, but Englishmen were inclined to rejoice at what struck them as an example of historic justice. For years the French had been fishing in troubled waters with Lafayette and the "Athletes of Liberty," carrying their swords to the service of England's rebels in the New World. The spectacle of those athletes carrying the American gospel of liberty to Paris was matter for a somewhat vindictive rejoicing. At least it would keep the old enemy too busy to trouble Europe for a while, since France had, as the British ambassador predicted, "too many distresses of Her own to admit of Her attempting at present to regain that ascendancy in the general balance to which she has before pretended." The French had likewise imagined some years earlier that perfidious Albion, too, would find herself impeded by domestic difficulties. In 1767, when Chatham's ministry was breaking down, Choiseul, the French minister of war and foreign affairs, wrote, "I hope that anarchy will prevail for some time. Indeed, I wish it would last a century." It was common enough for neighbors thus to rejoice at one another's troubles in these years of spreading revolution. Only the Younger Pitt, the prime minister who was in most respects a superior man, seems to have refrained. Despite the injury France had done Britain, he harbored no designs of revenge, but wished only to live in peace with her. As for the prospect of France acquiring an excess of strength from a reformed government, Pitt disclaimed alarm, for it was his duty as an Englishman, he said, to welcome every approximation to England's free and happy condition. In this he showed himself a great deal more liberal than those who were always professing their enlightenment. How childish, indeed wicked, were those who kept up the doctrine of natural and perpetual enmity between the two peoples, he said, in refuting the opposition's argument that the free-trade treaty with France in 1786 was giving arms to the enemies. Doctrines of perpetual or "natural" enmity between nations, he declared, were "a libel on the constitution of political societies," assuming "diabolical malice in the original frame of man."

This enlightened attitude reveals Pitt for what he was, and what his enemies, past and present, have denied him to be, one of the brightest stars of the eighteenth-century Enlightenment, a true child of his time at its best. "Depend upon it, Mr. Burke," he said as the Irishman was panicking about the spread of the French Revolution, "things will go on very much as they are until the Day of Judgment." "Aye," said Burke, "but it is the day of no judgment that I am worried about." It is said that Pitt lost a night's sleep but twice in his life—once when his friend Lord Melville was on the verge of impeachment, and again when Nelson was killed at Trafalgar, both highly personal crises. The notion that he was a bloodless pedant stirred only by abstract ideas, and those out of date, is one of the libels put upon him by foolish young men like Coleridge. His concern as prime minister was to safeguard England from bloody revolution, for the French Revolution was a world movement that struck France first. It was not, Edmund Burke perceived, "France extending a foreign empire over other nations: [it was] a sect aiming at universal empire, and beginning with the conquest of France." Burke was not exaggerating the magnitude of the event. The Revolution did conquer France as preliminary to the conquest of Europe, and the world at large. Whether this was to succeed entirely was what the long Revolutionary and Napoleonic Wars were about.

Matthew Arnold had the wisdom to see that political principles operate in different ways in different countries. "It seems to me," he wrote in his essay on democracy, "that one may save oneself from much idle terror at names and shadows if one will be at pains to remember what different conditions the different character of two nations must necessarily impose on the operation of any principle." And it was true that the noxious doctrines and practices of the French Revolution which issued in Jacobinism and the Reign of Terror, emerged in England in the form of a middle-class franchise, elementary education, and the industrial democracy of trade-unionism. The key words of the French Revolution—Liberty, Equality, Fraternity—were traced by undergraduates in gunpowder on the lawns of the colleges of Cambridge, but when they were ignited they drifted away in a fume of smoke, and the next shower

*Thomas Rowlandson's drawings of English nautical types include, clockwise, a purser, cook, cabin boy, and lieutenant.*

of rain extinguished the scorched lettering. After all, England had already had her revolution in the seventeenth century. All that the influence of the Revolution in France did was to score some of the old catchwords like Liberty more deeply into the minds as well as the grass, affording the skeptic a living proof that politics were not the prerogative or the privilege of property. Lower down the social scale workingmen foregathered in public houses to listen to the reading of Tom Paine and founded reform clubs with a subscription of a penny a week. The kind of question they wanted answered was why a man must work all the hours God gave and yet be unable to keep his wife and children from hunger.

Universal suffrage was one objective. Bread and cheese was another, since working-class politics in England from the start involved the basic question of food. "The rich want liberty, the poor want ham and eggs," was noticeably true long before the disciples of Karl Marx said it. The reason that ordinary men in England continued talking "the politics of liberty" instead of breaking the windows of bakers' shops (although sometimes they did that, too) was that they had behind them a long tradition of properly political activity and were used to translating economic concern into political terms. If they could improve the political setup, they believed, economic betterment could be brought about by act of parliament. Get the suffrage, their most influential leaders told them day in and day out, and all else shall be added unto you. Such was the teaching of William Cobbett and such was the belief of the Chartists, working-class proponents of political reforms to alleviate social distress. All through the nineteenth century working-class politics maintained this faith. Even now, with both universal suffrage and the welfare state a reality, the historian traces the genesis of both to the age of the French Revolution.

The first reaction of English opinion to that revolution was one of approval if not of enthusiasm. The French were to be congratulated upon catching up with their British neighbors in establishing a free government, and the foremost to offer their congratulations were Protestant dissenters like Dr. Richard Price, the Unitarian preacher at the Meeting House in the Old Jewry, whose sermon to the members of the Society for Commemorating the Revolution in Great Britain aroused Edmund Burke's ire and brought forth his *Reflections,* a book which had the impact of a deed rather than a bunch of printed pages, and which in its turn brought forth Tom Paine's *Rights of Man.* The thunder of the debate that these two initiated has not even now quite subsided. That the dissenters were in the forefront of the intellectual battle was the most important intellectual alignment in modern British history: it meant that the advocates of the Revolution in Great Britain were educated middle-class men of impeccable moral seriousness. These were the social and intellectual descendants of the Cromwellian radicals of the seventeenth century, and one of their earliest concerns was to reprint the literature of their ancestors, much of it republican.

The quality and the quantity of this literature remains astonishing. Where did its authors get their education? They were precluded by reason of their religious unorthodoxy from public schools and universities. They sent their sons to academies of their own foundation, places where practical subjects were taught in a practical way—living rather than dead languages, science rather than theology, everything that concerned the people on the earth rather than those underneath it. History? Yes, mainly modern. Mathematics? Say rather arithmetic, the summing of pounds, shillings, and pence rather than geometry or algebra. Out of the dissenting academies came that submerged segment of intellectual underworld, which constituted a fissure or cleavage in English society. Such men easily became adherents to programs of reform, for they had little or no stake in the existing order of corrupt boroughs, church livings, or profitable jobs dispensed by aristocratic patronage. Their reformism may have been that of an underworld, but it was not underhanded. There was nothing conspiratorial about it. It was frank, outspoken, ineffably decent. It invested liberal principles with moralism. It had a great deal to do with the respectability of English radicalism in a revolutionary age. More than anything else it saved England from infection from the violence of the French Revolution.

When England went to war (a war declared by France) with the French Revolution in 1793, the Younger Pitt insisted that her quarrel was not with French opinions but with French determination to impose opinions at the point of the bayonet, to give the law to Europe at the mouth of French cannon. To this England would never submit: she quickly became, as a French historian put it, "the one redoubtable adversary of the French Revolution because she alone could oppose to it

similar forces—national principles and popular passions." She could also oppose to it the armaments devised by the Industrial Revolution. Not that France had not also the output of modern industry; for years, English travelers like Arthur Young had been reporting the progress of the French armaments trade—the duke of Choiseul's steel manufactory at Amboise, and Wilkinson's factory for boring cannon by steam-driven machinery, also on the Loire—and it was well known to British shipbuilders that if the navy wanted the best ships of the line they must capture them from the French. 

But in the early years of George III's reign, John Roebuck had founded the Carron Ironworks. By 1796 it had an output of more than five thousand tons, and its name had become a household word throughout Europe with the fame of its carronades, the small and handy cannons that, mounted on Nelson's ships of the line, did more than any other weapon to bring Great Britain naval supremacy, as may be judged by Napoleon's constant cry for more carronades. Names like Wilkinson and Watt, Rennie and Roebuck, stand amidst clouds of steam behind the glorious figure of Nelson. And when we speak of the part played by national principles and popular passions in bringing victory we must not forget for a moment the people of the two extremes of Europe, Russia and the Iberian Peninsula. Great Britain's contribution to the land war was late in getting under way, but it was the British infantry which finally broke Napoleon, "the Man who was more than a man," on the bloody battlefields of Spain and Belgium.

In the twenty years' war during which Great Britain was France's most persistent and redoubtable enemy, there was little to be said of the British as a fighting people except that they refused to give in. They fought the French not only because they consciously held a different ideology, but because the French were the ancient enemy of Agincourt and Crécy, and their beastly next-door neighbors. As G. K. Chesterton put it,

*We lay in blazing ruins,*
*Fighting and fearing not*
*The strange fierce face of the Frenchman*
*Who knew for what he fought.*

To imagine that the English soldier also knew what he was fighting

*Three of the flagships commanded by Admiral Nelson, Lord of the Fleet*

for would be to attribute to him an intellectual power that he certainly lacked. Questioned about it, he would doubtless have replied not for what, but rather for *whom,* he fought—for the good old king, George III, or for Old Nosey, the duke of Wellington. The latter was under no illusions in that matter; neither was Nelson, who always referred to the French as "those fellows," a people especially created in order to be "thrashed" by the British.

Napoleon once said that an English army under French officers could conquer the earth, and by this he probably referred to the inability of the rank and file to know when it was beaten. When Napoleon came up against peoples in arms, in Spain and in Russia, he met his match, and there was always something of that equation about his British opponents, more especially about the British navy. Nelson's navy was the darling of the nation. It had—and knew it had—the people behind it as the army rarely did. "The scum of the earth enlisted for drink," was what the duke of Wellington called the army which fought for him so magnificently.

When the long war was over, the English remained true to form. They wanted to withdraw from the field and live the civilized life again, while their Continental allies endeavored to persuade them to remain an active participant in Europe. After so long and effective a partnership in the coalitions against Napoleon, the British could hardly withdraw completely and suddenly from the European community. And yet they were inclined to regard the Continent rather as the United States viewed it after the peace of Versailles in 1919—that is, as the home of ancient tyrannies and corruption. They did not wish to be involved in its affairs any more than was absolutely necessary for their own security. When Czar Alexander tried to turn the Quadruple Alliance of the Great Powers into a Holy Alliance—a kind of monarchical trade union for running the affairs of Europe in the interests of kings and the *status quo*—he succeeded in securing the adherence of everyone except Turkey and Great Britain. The former was excluded anyway because she was not Christian; the latter stood aside ostensibly because her king, George III, was mad, but in fact because Lord Castlereagh, the foreign minister, suspected the whole plan as being a device for minding everybody else's business. England, after all, owed her reigning family to a revolution—that of 1688—so how could she be other than lukewarm toward counterrevolutionary plans hatched by despotic rulers for the suppression of revolutionary movements in Italy and Spain? "We shall be found in our place when actual danger menaces the system of Europe," Castlereagh assured the monarchs in 1820, "but this country cannot and will not act upon Speculative Principles of Precaution."

After Castlereagh's death, his successor George Canning withdrew his country altogether from her equivocal association with the despots, and it was his continuation of Castlereagh's policy of nonintervention that strengthened President Monroe's hand in the promulgation of his Doctrine in 1824 at the time the South American republics established their independence of Spain. This policy of friendly neutrality toward peoples struggling for national freedom and independence governed British foreign policy throughout the nineteenth century. It was an attitude that consorted well with a great industrial country's interest in overseas markets. Profit and power, idealism and investments, were never far apart in the age of the French and the Industrial Revolutions, or in any other revolutionary age.

CHAPTER IX

# VICTORIAN ENGLAND

The long war ended appropriately with Napoleon surrendering to British naval officers on board H.M.S. *Bellerophon,* a first-rate man-of-war bearing the honorable scars of the Nile and Trafalgar. England had been at war for twenty-two years, and she emerged a good deal richer and more powerful than victorious powers generally contrive to emerge from modern wars, by reason of her superior naval power, by her success in collaring the colonies of her ally, Holland, and also by hanging on to the lion's share of the world's trade. Yet she had a considerable backlog of problems that had been neglected or postponed in the stress of war.

The first of these in magnitude and urgency arose out of a great increase of population, amounting to what our own age would call an explosion. There had been a 40 per cent increase during the second half of the eighteenth century, followed by a 50 per cent increase in the first three decades of the nineteenth. The total jump from 6,500,000 to 14,000,000 was not in itself frightening, for, as people said, "with every mouth God sends a pair of hands." The frightening thing was the industrial town, in which many of these people were living, a new

*The houses of parliament, completed in 1860 in the neo-Gothic style*

phenomenon in history—dark, mysterious, full of unknown social menace. It was an age of optimism about technical improvement, vaguely called progress, but of increasing pessimism about human survival. Pessimism, deep despondency, was especially evoked by the publication in 1798 of Thomas Malthus' *Essay on the Principle of Population,* predicting that the number of humans would outstrip food supplies in the near future if growth rates went on as they had in recent times.

Malthus intended to create pessimism, being tired of his father's talk of the marquis de Condorcet's theory of the ultimate perfectibility of mankind. No one in his senses imagined that government could do much about it, although there were dreadful hints about putting down poison for the infant population, setting up "parish exterminators," and suchlike horrors. It fell to government to take steps to feed and house these millions, if only to stop them from cutting the throats of their masters. The problem of population came home to the authorities in terms of law and order, sanitation, public health, elementary education. These problems were referred to under the collective heading of the Condition of England Question, and with the coming of peace they could no longer be evaded.

Indeed, the greater part of social legislation throughout the nineteenth century was concerned with ameliorating the lot of the poor, often amidst a great deal of class hatred or rancor. Fear of revolution had never died out since the French Revolution, and conditions seemed especially favorable to social upheaval in an industrial society like England. The alternatives were grim, for to prevent the poor from dying of starvation seemed to many people a mistaken policy, aggravating the problem of numbers and their pressure upon food supplies. The only answer, thought some, including Malthus himself, lay in moral restraint, so that fewer children were born, and that consequently fewer (of the poor, of course) went on living. No wonder political economy became known as the dismal science. Not that such arguments had any great effect; the Victorian period was distinguished in England as a time of large families, especially among the clergy and the poor. The upper classes had always practiced birth control, but an age and society of puritan moral teaching regarded discussion of the topic with horror.

What Thomas Hardy called the "strenuous race," emerging victorious from the Napoleonic Wars, was not greatly dismayed by the prob-

*English curiosity seekers row out to the* Bellerophon *to see Napoleon.*

lems confronting it. Above all, the nation believed in itself. After defeating the most powerful country on earth under the greatest conqueror of modern times, Englishmen were unlikely to quail before the rhetoric of parlor radicals or before a handful of machine-wreckers, who hoped by such destruction to restore some human balance to production. During the years just before and just after Waterloo, workmen for the industrial centers of England staged riots. Known as Luddites, these impassioned protesters systematically destroyed the machinery to which they attributed the prevailing lack of employment. In 1812 there were as many troops on foot in England as had gone to the Peninsular War under Wellington. The government made machine-breaking a capital offense, abolished the income tax in accordance with Pitt's promise when he had imposed it strictly as a wartime measure, and after Waterloo passed a corn law restricting imported grain in order to keep up the price of the home-grown product in the interests of agriculture. By the Combination Acts of 1799–1800, workers were prohibited from forming trade unions, which were deemed "conspiracies in restraint of trade."

On the whole, however, the fashionable political economy taught that the best way to encourage things to get back to normal again was to refrain from legislative interference. Almost everyone accepted as gospel the teaching of Adam Smith's *Inquiry into the Nature and Causes of the Wealth of Nations* (1776). *Laissez faire, laissez passer* (no interference, complete freedom of movement) was the rule. "Men cannot create abundance where Providence has inflicted scarcity," Henry Addington, the Home secretary, would tell the House of Commons, and all through the century a great deal of ingenuity was needed to make a case for interference of the state in economic matters. Factory acts or the most elementary laws to protect women and children from industrial exploitation required long and subtle argumentation. The onus of proof, it was believed in those days, rested upon those who wanted change, not on those who wished to resist it, and most people believed with Lord Falkland that "when it is not necessary to change, it is necessary not to change." They felt no call to apologize for their inertia.

It is extraordinary how little difference a great deal of energy made. For instance, after much agitation a parliamentary reform bill was passed in 1832, which the duke of Wellington imagined might lead to revolution by admitting to the franchise male persons living in houses worth ten pounds a year rental (that is, those possessing a minimal amount of property); yet all he found to say when he met the new House of Commons was that he had never seen "such a lot of shocking bad hats," referring to the dissolute membership. From the point of view of democracy, or government of the people, by the people, for the people—which was what people like Wellington most feared—it made hardly any difference in the composition or character of parliament at the time, even if it did pave the way to universal suffrage in the course of a century or so. The fact is that the aristocracy, great and small, that had governed England for so long, had decided, or been compelled, to admit a tiny section of the middle class to a share in decision making. But if it is true, as Mirabeau said, *administrer, c'est gouverner,* then the aristocracy still governed, for it is very certain that they held all the keys of administration. By his reforms at Rugby School—both in a serious attitude toward scholarship and in the responsibility of boys for the government of boys through the headmaster's relationships with the sixth form—Dr. Thomas Arnold equipped the upper classes for the tasks of administration. One testimonial accompanying his application for the post at Rugby had predicted that "if Mr. Arnold were elected, he would change the face of education all through the public schools of England." His influence on education in those schools was indeed profound, and he thereby ensured that government in England would remain where it had always been, whatever changes might take place in the franchise and however far education might be extended down the social scale.

Entering upon the forty years of peace which was to last until the Crimean War in 1854, the country was in a position to put its house in order without constant anxiety about national stability, and it may be doubted whether any society has ever submitted itself to the unremitting and searching scrutiny that England underwent in the decades immediately before and after 1832. There were royal commissions of inquiry into almost everything; a great amount of evidence was taken under oath and submitted in reports which parliament ordered to be published as "blue books." These might or might not be acted upon in legislation, but often they formed the basis of novels, such as Disraeli's

*Sybil* and Kingsley's *Water Babies,* thereby reaching a much wider reading public than if they had remained merely official publications. These facts and figures did much to stimulate the growth of a social conscience to an unpredictable degree.

The coming of the railways brought all parts of the country into close contact with one another, making it possible for people of different social classes to see with their own eyes how the others lived, long before the illustrated press came into existence. Steam trains began to run regularly in 1830. The reign of Queen Victoria became known as the Age of Equipoise, even the Age of Complacency, although it was never thought of in such terms by the people who lived at the time. Rather the Victorian Englishman seems to have been conscious of living in a period of acute and constant danger and disturbance. In 1842 Tennyson spoke for his age and its anxieties in "Locksley Hall":

> *Slowly comes a hungry people, as a lion creeping nigher,*
> *Glares at one that nods and winks behind a slowly-dying fire.*

He not only celebrated the railway as a symbol of progress: "Let the great world spin for ever down the ringing grooves of change"; he also gave his readers an ominous glimpse of air warfare: "Heard the heavens fill with shouting, and there rain'd a ghastly dew/From the nations' airy navies grappling in the central blue." One way or another, Victorian England had its fair share of grim apprehension, with its scientific imaginings and its practical experience of the crowded and unhygienic life of humanity in such conurbations as Liverpool and Manchester and Birmingham, where the life of a city floated on a sea of sewage, and a poor widow infected hundreds of her neighbors with cholera, in order, Carlyle grimly gibed, to prove that "we are all members one of another." It is when the poor infected their "betters," it has been noted, that the upper classes began to take the cause of public health seriously, and cholera was no respector of persons.

Many of England's chief glories have been achieved under her queens—Elizabeth I, Anne, Victoria. The men of an essentially romantic race seem especially touched to high endeavor in the service of a woman. "I have fallen hopelessly in love with the Queen," the young Charles Dickens wrote at the time of Victoria's nuptials in 1840. Nor was he simply playing the fool. The same heroine whom Benjamin

Disraeli thirty years later called privately the Fairy was very much a woman in her predilections and otherwise among her ministers. The rather wooden rectitude of Sir Robert Peel and the no less priggish and unbending manner of Gladstone prevented her from regarding their great public services with enthusiasm. Peel's lowering of the price of food by his repeal of the Corn Laws in 1846, and his founding of an unpolitical and unarmed police force in an age of often embittered class warfare, did much to preserve the peace of Victorian England. Gladstone tried for many years, and at a great cost to the unity of his party, to meet the clamor of the Irish for Home Rule.

It was during the ministry of the avuncular Lord Melbourne—Victoria's "Dear Lord M."—that two measures which were to have a great

*A convivial gathering in the drawing room of Saint James Palace*

impact on the daily lives of the people were introduced: penny postage, and state-aided education. In these years, too, Gladstone's work as chancellor of the Exchequer established a wholesome tradition that the money of the people is best left to fructify in the people's pockets, though it has been much disregarded since. There was evidently imaginative statesmanship in plenty when Victoria was queen, and Great Britain showed the world that a people may be great through economical domestic policies as much as by the sword. Victorian England was by no means a pacific community, but it certainly bore out Milton's aphorism in praise of Cromwell: "Peace hath her victories no less renowned than war."

The queen's husband, Albert, the prince consort, did more for the arts than for art, presiding over the great display of manufactures in 1851 known as the Great Exhibition, held at the Crystal Palace in Hyde Park (later transferred to Sydenham). That extraordinary building, which Colonel Sibthorpe predicted in the House of Commons would (he hoped and prayed) draw down the wrath of God in a splintering catastrophe, was designed by Joseph Paxton, celebrated architect and horticulturist who was chief gardener to the duke of Devonshire at Chatsworth, and it was to withstand the elements and pecking sparrows and roaring choirs for long enough to serve as a memorial to the technical achievements of Victorian England. (The image of the prince consort, its great patron, still stands in his own memorial in Hyde Park, holding, presumably, the catalogue of the exhibition in his hand.) The Crystal Palace was 1,848 feet long and some 400 feet wide. With its glittering glass galleries and transepts framed in cast iron it was the Victorian counterpart of the medieval cathedral, celebrating the god of material progress. It was almost as splendid a pledge of the nation's faith in the future as the monumental proportions of Euston Station, the railroad terminus that had been created thirteen years earlier. The exhibition was opened by the queen, who drove with the royal family from Buckingham Palace, on the first of May, amidst scenes of great enthusiasm. There were no soldiers and hardly a policeman in sight on that happy day, and the prophets of woe who had predicted disorders, even revolution, in the capital with the assembly of multitudes (there were 25,000 spectators) were amply confounded. Day after day throughout that splendid summer the people came,

43,000 a day, by excursion trains from all over England, six million in all, consuming three million pennybuns and a million bottles of mineral water ("NO INTOXICANTS"), and the conduct of the crowds was exemplary: they shook hands with strangers and shed tears of satisfaction. They sang *The Allelujah Chorus* at the opening and *God Save the Queen* at the slightest provocation. Why? What did the Great Exhibition stand for? It symbolized the social unity and harmony of Victorian England, the end of the alarm and rancor that had dominated class relationships for at least a generation of industrial life.

Karl Marx, the great celebrant of class war, was hard at work in that seedbed of revolution—the reading room of the British Museum—where he would spend the last thirty years of his life writing *Das Kapital.* Did the Great Exhibition help foster his unfailing enthusiasm for the productive achievements of capitalism, even while he lamented its distributive injustices? Marx predicted that the land of his studious exile would prove the birthplace of the first socialist society as it had been the birthplace of the Industrial Revolution, and he still quietly awaits it on Highgate Hill where his bones are buried. He had not believed that capitalism could go on indefinitely making concessions to the working class without collapsing of its internal contradictions. More than a hundred years have passed, and it is still doing so—without turning England into a fascist monster in order to protect its ill-gotten gains, save in the imaginations of Marx's imaginative grandchildren. That is, perhaps, the most remarkable achievement of Victorian England, the great age of concession.

The Crystal Palace horrified not only Colonel Sibthorpe. An Oxford undergraduate named William Morris was discovered prostrate on a seat in Hyde Park, struck down by the vision of such a monstrosity perpetrated in the land of Chaucer and Shakespeare, not to mention John Ruskin. Ruskin himself protested against the notion that "a greenhouse larger than any greenhouse was built before" had any artistic significance, however great its mechanical ingenuity. Instead of such an "entirely novel order of architecture" which set up pillars of cast-iron and panels of glass, he said, what was needed was the rescue of beautiful old buildings from the hands of the vandals and the "restorer." Twenty years later, William Morris and his friends founded the Society for the Protection of Ancient Buildings or, as they nick-

named it, the Anti-Scrape Society, to prevent the removal of the patina from old stone. One of Ruskin's proposals, made in a pamphlet "On the Opening of the Crystal Palace," was to save ancient buildings by buying them for the nation. This was the germ of the National Trust, a body that has taken into its keeping many of the best and most beautiful buildings of the English past. Some of these, often with their contents, have been accepted by the state in lieu of death duties, alleviating the appalling injustice which may follow a succession of taxes and lead to the ruin of ancient and honorable families, even when the deaths occur in the nation's service.

The foundation of such organizations for the protection of the nation's inheritance was symptomatic of the nineteenth century's devotion

*Slums, like the ones in Gustave Doré's engraving, became a permanent blight on the English industrial landscape of the 1800s.*

to the past. The popular genius of such writers as Carlyle and Macaulay and John Richard Green made history a cult, almost a passion. Perhaps this is something that happens when a people are growing old. Compared with such ancient societies as Greece and Rome, Egypt and China, England was still youthful in terms of years, but age has to be measured in terms of historical experience. The Protestant Reformation, the scientific revolution of the seventeenth century, the Industrial Revolution of the eighteenth and nineteenth—all these and more lie at the root of the modern English state, like layers of leaf mold around the roots of a tree. Twice in the last years of Victoria's reign the English people celebrated a royal jubilee with pomp and circumstance. Since that time they have not merely recited Kipling's *Recessional* with its recurrent refrain of "Lest We Forget"; they have lived in its terms, forsaking empire for gentler ways, and the Empire has given way to the Commonwealth. No other imperial people in history have changed course and direction so certainly and with so little fuss. It was a Victorian historian who spoke of England's having acquired an empire in a fit of absent-mindedness, and there certainly has been a degree of somnambulism about her manner of resigning it. It took a novelist to express the truth about that, and about much else in her history. In *To Be a Pilgrim,* the late Joyce Cary spoke of England as "born upon the road" and living "in such a dust of travel that she never knows where she is. . . ." "She is the wandering Dutchman," he said, "the pilgrim and the scapegoat of the world. . . ." A sublime somnambulist? A gypsy? History's Flying Dutchman? Cary was writing in 1942, and events since that time have lent force to his closing paragraphs, where he likens England to "one or two other peoples of similar stock, history, etc., who are also apt to find themselves in new lodgings at short notice. . . ."

Histories of the reign of Queen Victoria have traditionally contained chapters not on the British Empire but on "Britain Overseas." That is how the Victorians preferred to speak of "the Empire on which the sun never sets," consisting as it did of settlements of the English (and the Irish and the Scots) in distant lands. Over all those settlements, in jungle clearings, on the banks of eastern rivers, on veldt and prairie, beside blue lagoons and sunny seas where palm and pine waved like distant banners in the wind, the Union Jack was hoisted in the breeze

of morning and lowered to the salute of the evening gun. The schoolboy was told he should be proud of it, although in fact he found it a rather tedious geography lesson. What he enjoyed was the tale of heroic personalities, each of whom, it seemed, had begun as an English schoolboy and each of whom, it seemed, had "made good." He was encouraged to emulate such lads as Jim Harris, the future Lord Malmesbury, and British ambassador at the Hague, Berlin, and Saint Petersburg. Jim was brought up in the cathedral close at Salisbury, where his mother was walking one day when she chanced to observe a small figure, which from a distance looked as small as a fly, climbing up the spire. Borrowing a spyglass, Mrs. Harris dropped it in terror when she perceived that the "fly" was her James, a schoolboy, on his way to the top. The Victorian youth was also given the adventure stories of George A. Henty, nearly all of which bore a title patterned on *With Clive in India.* He was brought up on real-life tales of English heroes, just as his American cousins eagerly read stories of "from log-cabin to White House," or the life of President Garfield. So with the makers of England's industrial fortunes, for the success story was the favorite Victorian fiction. Matthew Arnold was fond of quoting the story that Sir Daniel Gooch, chairman of the Great Western Railway, used to tell his workmen at Swindon: "Ever remember, my dear Dan," Mrs. Gooch used to repeat to her son every morning as he set out to his work, "that you should look forward to being some day manager of that concern." This, said Arnold, was the Victorian version of the golden rule, or the divine injunction "Be ye Perfect" done into British.

This same legend of youthful enterprise and intrepidity hung about the early years of all the great entrepreneurs of the Industrial Revolution, men like Richard Arkwright, Josiah Wedgwood, Robert Owen, and a host of others. The century when the Empire was made, as well as the factories and the power-driven machinery, was perfectly adapted to the rise of the heroic figure. Never had such scope for man's will to power existed before; the conditions of the time were ideal. There was no compulsory education to detain a boy from active life until he had lost his freshness and acquired the dull habits of scholastic life. Government, too, let him alone. It was not until well into the nineteenth century that legislation laid down any rules of the game such as the detailed provisions of patent law. A bright young man at that time

*Queen Victoria in 1876, the year she became empress of India*

could pick anyone's brains and get rich quick. It was not a matter of a small number of smart alecks enslaving the rest, but of many lively lads letting loose their energies into new and enticing fields of adventure.

The spirit in which the empire builders went about their work was typical of a mercantile society. They did not go overseas like the Romans in order to extend an *imperium;* the empire they established was a concessionary one. They went for the profits of trade, and when they established a colony under their country's flag, it was called a factory—a word whose primary dictionary meaning is "a merchant company's foreign trading station," and only secondarily a "manufactory"; just as a merchant buying and selling on commission is the dictionary meaning of "factor." Sooner or later such traders and adventurers had to be afforded military assistance by their home government, especially if they were flying their country's flag. That was how British power was established and extended in the Indian subcontinent. Yet the British government was generally reluctant to assume the burden of protecting, or in any way vindicating, the goings-on of the private company that had enjoyed the monopoly of trade in India and the Far East since 1609, when it was first chartered as the East India Company. Even Pitt the Elder, perhaps the greatest name in British imperialism, hesitated to take on responsibility for the company, which was referred to like a great person by the name of John Company. It was easy for private men to say glibly, "nationalize it," but quite apart from the responsibilities involved, there were to be considered the vast moral and social consequences of Oriental wealth. Chatham himself, speaking on the state of the nation in the House of Lords in 1770, referred to the "influx of wealth into this country which has been attended by many fatal consequences, because it has not been the regular, natural product of labor and industry. The riches of Asia," he continued, "have poured in upon us, and have brought with them not only Asiatic luxury, but I fear Asiatic principles of government. Without connections, without any natural interest in the soil, the importers of foreign gold have forced their way into parliament by such a torrent of private corruption as no private hereditary fortune could resist. . . . The corruption of the people is the great original cause of the discontents of the people themselves . . . and the notorious decay of the internal vigor of the constitution." It was a high price to pay for commercial monopoly.

*Strollers browse among some 1,500 display cases filled with goods from around the world at London's Crystal Palace.*

*Cargo ships in the Napoleonic era dock in the harbor at Calcutta, capital of British India until 1912.*

Step by step, however, the government was driven to accept responsibility for the dominion with which a trading empire had saddled the country. By the reign of Queen Victoria, and even earlier, the concessional was giving place to the territorial empire. It was no longer a matter of British merchants going out and securing trade concessions from native rulers and setting up outposts which might be required to be defended by British troops, as well as by the private army of "John Company" if they got into difficulties. Instead, it became a matter of extensive areas on the world map being painted red. The whole was known as the British Empire, which had its own minister of the Crown, known as Her Majesty's secretary for the colonies, with a seat in the cabinet and an ornate office in Whitehall.

Robert Clive had been a clerk in the East India Company factory at Madras and had become a highly successful soldier in the defense of its outposts and the overthrow of its French rivals in the subcontinent. It is true that he made a fortune out of his career, and when a parliamentary committee examined him in later life he complained that he had been treated like a sheepstealer. As for the charge that he laid hands on the treasure of the native princes, he protested, "By God, Mr. Chairman, at this moment I stand astonished by my own moderation!" Like many another servant of the company he learned financial shadiness from his employers. The company actually encouraged its servants to pay themselves by trading privately, although the practice was formally prohibited. It also did its best to ruin a man's moral character by overloading him with authority and its accompanying temptations. When Clive won India, the most the British government could claim to have contributed was the dispatch of meager royal forces to co-operate with those of the company in defense of its possessions, and a certain amount of naval support. William Pitt never allowed India to distract him from the conquest of Canada, but furthermore he knew he could leave the task to the company and its "Heaven-born general," Robert Clive. Clive has been called a sort of Henry VIII of Asia, and it must be said that he looked it, with his small eyes between puffy lids, his great straddling bulk, and his domineering manner. Like many of his fellows he was addicted much to opium. His statue in the hall of East India House in Leadenhall Street showed him in a Roman toga, and this was not inappropriate, for as one historian has remarked, the

*Baron Robert Clive seized the province of Bengal from the natives in the 1750s and installed himself as its governor.*

 original pirate king was in due course replaced by the proconsul.

Clive's successor was the most remarkable proconsul England ever produced. As the first governor general under Lord North's Regulating Act of 1773, Warren Hastings in little more than ten years laid down the permanent principles of British rule in India and did more for the ultimate benefit of the people of the subcontinent than any man of his century and most men since. "Thousands reaping the benefits [of his rule] offer up their prayers for the prosperity of England and for the success of the Company," the people of Murshedabad in Bengal declared, but Warren Hastings was rewarded at home by impeachment for corruption and misrule. The impeachment dragged on for seven years, and cost Hastings his whole fortune before acquittal. He was

represented as a tyrant and a monster of cruelty because he was resolute, vigorous, and highhanded in emergency, in fact a benevolent despot, exercising what amounted to absolute authority over peoples who understood no other. His impeachment, while conducted with a good deal of self-righteousness by Edmund Burke, can never be wholly deplored since it brought out what badly needed to be brought out in the government of India—that is, that moral qualities must inform the behavior of a dominant race invested with supreme authority. While we are sorry for the man who incurred the blame for a long course of exploitation of one people by another—especially in view of his own long labors for the people of India—we cannot regret that his impeachment, coming so soon after the British mishandling of the American colonists, upheld standards of conduct which needed to be upheld unswervingly for as long as colonialism continued to exist. Whatever defects in British rule may have been responsible for the Indian Mutiny in 1858, that dark event had little or nothing to do with oppression of the subject people by their rulers. The fact was that the British government had injured too many sacred cows, not only by using cow-grease for oiling cartridges, but by the introduction of railways and telegraphs. Britain had mistaken Indian villagers for Victorian English peasant-proprietors on their way to becoming a bourgeoisie. She learned painfully that she must rule Indian people with respect for their traditional customs, however unenlightened they might be considered. After the mutiny the wise policy was followed of ruling India through her own most influential classes and not through academic notions of what India should be but was not.

To the Victorians, India was never imagined to be a part of "Britain Overseas," like Canada and Australia and New Zealand, whose territories were populated by people of predominantly British, or at least European, descent. India always remained what she was often called openly—"an English barrack in the Oriental seas"—a rich source of wealth and manpower, without which Britain has shrunk to become a European offshore island with a hard living to make in a hard world. The possession of India, "the brightest jewel in the imperial Crown," may be said to have sheltered her from most of the misfortunes which afflict small and impoverished peoples.

*Emancipate your Colonies!* was the title of Jeremy Bentham's book

*The unwarranted impeachment trial of Warren Hastings in the 1790s*

 of 1793; Richard Cobden called them "gorgeous and ponderous appendages to swell our ostensible grandeur without improving our balance of trade"; and Disraeli was saying, in 1852, "these wretched colonies will all be independent in a few years and are a millstone round our necks." Yet so greatly did opinion about such possessions change in Victorian times that both Canada and Australia became cherished nations on their way to that "equal partnership" with Britain which was to be described in the Balfour Definition of 1926. It had been proposed for long enough that the British Empire should be provided with a constitution. By 1926 there was an effective substitute for one in the Balfour Definition, which described the position and mutual relation of Great Britain and the dominions as follows: "They are autonomous Communities within the British Empire, equal in status, in no way subordinate one to another in any aspect of their domestic or external affairs though united by a common allegiance to the Crown and freely associated as members of the British Commonwealth of Nations."

Africa alone was the outstanding exception in this harmonious story and requires separate consideration. It was the Dark Continent until late in the nineteenth century, when there took place what is ingloriously described as the scramble for Africa. How the British came to acquire their considerable share of the continent is still somewhat mysterious; but by the 1880s they had occupied Egypt and staked out a huge tropical empire, although India and the British Isles were still regarded as the twin centers of their wealth and strength. Not until rather late were they interested in Africa per se; earlier the continent had been seen as a convenient location for coastal stations for communications with more distant lands. Opinions about its value ranged from that of James Stephen of the Colonial Office who took the view, in 1840, that "if we could acquire the Dominions of the whole of that Continent it would be but a worthless possession," to vague ideas that it might some day turn out to be another Australia or Canada. Nevertheless an African empire was acquired by the later years of Victoria's reign. Much to the sardonic jesting of other nations, the British clothed their national interests in African matters in the garb of Christian endeavor for the suppression of the slave trade and the propagation of the gospel among the heathen. The conjunction of bibles and brandy and gunpowder seems never to have proved a subject for mirth to the trueborn Englishman. For most it was a matter of moral concern. 

British imperialism reached its final and most flagrant phase in Africa when it produced Cecil Rhodes. It was as if the sordid and yet heroic tale of British empire building had to leave the world its own parody before it passed away forever. Rhodes, the son of an English parson, had been sent out to South Africa for his health at sixteen; after staking a claim in the newly opened diamond fields of Kimberley, at twenty he went home and entered Oxford, which was his first and last love. (He had gone to the diamond fields not only with a digger's outfit but with a number of classical texts and a lexicon; later he would spend some thousands of pounds having the authorities of Gibbon's *Decline and Fall* translated into English.) Returning to Africa, he developed new British territories to the west and north of the Transvaal, brought Rhodesia into existence, and saw an opportunity to establish a link with the regions beyond the Zambezi River, where David Livingstone and other missionaries had found the way into central Africa. Perhaps the grandest dream Rhodes had was of a railway from the Cape to Cairo.

This extraordinary man, who was only forty-eight when he died, struggling to breathe in the African heat, had a passion for making his will. At least six of them survive, all concerned to devote his very large fortune to the promotion of his lifelong passion—the bringing of the whole civilized world under British rule, as well as recovering the United States and making the Anglo-Saxon race into one empire. (One way he proposed to further this aim was by founding the Rhodes Scholarships.) As Rhodes wrote in his final testament, "I contend that we are the first race in the world and that the more of the world we inhabit, the better it is for the human race." It was an attitude that prompted one of his biographers to remark that the only sane provision in Rhodes' will was that it should not be opened until after his death.

Rhodes wanted to reconcile the British and Dutch in Africa, but he succeeded only in alienating them and provoking the Boer War. The country's humiliation in that unhappy conflict may be said to have cured the English of highhanded imperialism. The future, it could be seen, lay not with the Empire but with the Commonwealth. It is the only case in history of a great empire transforming itself into a gentler and more viable association of men.

CHAPTER X

# THE TWENTIETH CENTURY

After Nelson and Trafalgar the British navy ceased to count its victories. In the future, as young officers were fond of saying, a fellow in search of promotion must jump into the muzzle of a gun and crawl out of the touch hole where the powder was ignited. Mr. Midshipman Easy and the men of Captain Marryat's novels had to make their own opportunities for adventure and renown. Such is the peculiar inconvenience of being born in a heroic age. After Trafalgar, the navy did not fight another great naval action until Jutland in 1916—one hundred and eleven years later—for there was no one left at sea to fight. Instead, the British navy undertook the often invidious task of maintaining the *Pax Britannica,* which was not a matter of policing the oceans of the world but rather of "showing the flag" at trouble spots.

There were a number of other cogent reasons why the European powers engaged in so few major wars for a hundred years. But as time went on the English came to believe, if not to say, that the preponderance of their naval power was essential to the peace and well-being of the world. True, it was the ubiquity of the British man-of-war that enabled them to cherish their favorite image of themselves as the cham-

*Coventry Cathedral, built on the ruins of the old bombed-out church* pion of small nations struggling to be free. From the days of George Canning—that is, from the 1820s—onward, they patronized libertarian movements in the Old World and the New, not only in the establishment of South American republics winning their independence from Spain, but in the effective enforcement of the Monroe Doctrine by the United States, for, as it was said, American cockleboats followed in the wake of the British man-of-war. In Europe itself it was the watchful and "favorably neutral" attitude of the royal navy that made sure of the establishment of an independent and neutralized Belgium in 1830 and a united Italy in 1860.

Most, if not all, of such achievements of national independence were very much to the advantage of Great Britain and her commerce, as well as in the interest of the people concerned. It is significant that when the English economist Harriet Martineau wrote her *History of England during the Thirty Years' Peace* in 1846–49, she entered almost at once into a fifty-page account of the new South American republics with a detailed map and a portrait of Simon Bolívar. This was a part of the world, she said, "which unfolded prospects in the highest degree interesting to our country in particular."

A policeman's lot is not a happy one, and it took the English a considerable time to realize how unpopular their nineteenth-century role had made them in the world at large. They undoubtedly acquired an unenviable reputation for smugness, deceit, and hypocrisy. "This island was Blest, sir," Charles Dickens has Mr. Podsnap explain to a "foreign gentleman" in *Our Mutual Friend,* his great satire on Victorian humbug, "to the Direct Exclusion of such Other Countries as—as there may happen to be. And if we were all Englishmen present I would say . . . that there is in the Englishman a combination of qualities, a modesty, an independence, a responsibility, a repose, combined with an absence of everything calculated to call a blush into the cheek of a young person, which one would seek in vain among the Nations of the Earth." This is very obviously satire directed at the English by an Englishman. What the English themselves failed to realize was that the dislike aroused by such traits would become lethal hatred when England's hour of peril should arrive. That hour did arrive in the later years of the century, when the world once more became a dangerous place with the rise of a jealous and highly militarized Germany. England's ancient enemy was France, and France had been defeated by Prussia in the process of uniting Germany under her leadership in the Franco-Prussian War of 1870.

English liberals like John Stuart Mill suffered acute misgivings at the prospect of German hegemony, and believed that Britain should have intervened to prevent it, not for the love of the old enemy but for the maintenance of that traditional British interest, the balance of power in Europe. At the time, however, the British preferred to believe that France was the aggressor, and that the Germans were generally to be preferred to the French on moral grounds. There was something unreliable, not to say immoral, about the French, whereas the Germans were generally referred to as "our German cousins," people of a kindred stock. After all, Germany was the homeland not only of the original English race but of Queen Victoria and Albert the Good. It was the land of most of the things the Victorians loved—Christmas trees, Christmas cards, red-cheeked children, smiling peasants, hearty beer-drinking merchants, meerschaum-smoking professors, the German waiter, the German band, the innocent jollity of the German *Festspiel.* Only after 1914 did the Englishman begin to suspect that the German waiter, the German band, the German Herr professor had been serving the German fatherland as spies; the phrase "Made in Germany" on cheap imported goods became as hateful as "Made in Japan" was to become in some quarters at a later date. German industrial competition was unfair competition, it was argued, because the German worker worked too hard and was paid too little.

The turning point in Anglo-German relations had come in 1896, when Kaiser Wilhelm II intervened in a family quarrel by congratulating President Kruger of the Transvaal for having rounded up a British invading force led by Dr. Starr Jameson. The notorious Jameson Raid has become the prototype of the piratical politics with which the world has become familiar in the twentieth century; it resembles the lawless techniques employed by Hitler's Germany in seeking to disrupt a weaker neighbor, as with Czechoslovakia on the eve of World War II. The Boer inhabitants of the Transvaal, a society of Bible-reading farmers descended from the Dutch colony taken over by the British after the Napoleonic Wars, wanted to be left alone to exploit the land and the black folk beyond the Vaal River, something the British settlers

were reluctant to allow, especially after the discovery of rich deposits of gold there. Paul Kruger and his farmers of the Transvaal generally detested the British settlers (whom they called *Uitlanders,* or outsiders) and the latter came to feel themselves an oppressed minority. Dr. Jameson and his six-hundred-man invading force were posing as "liberators" of the *Uitlanders* when they were captured and rounded up, to the applause of Britain's enemies everywhere, and especially in Germany. When, after being returned to London for trial, they got away with very light penalties, it did not require great prescience to foresee the Boer War, which began in 1899. English historians often consider this to have been the first chapter of the Anglo-German conflict which occupied the first half of the present century, even though Germany was not officially involved. Looking back, Winston Churchill was to write, "I date the beginning of these violent times in our country from the Jameson Raid."

*The H.M.S.* Furious, *British Dreadnought in World War I, from which the first ship-based attack was launched in 1917*

Queen Victoria died in the middle of the South African War, and her death, more truly than the death of most royal figures, was the end of an era. She died when the English were suffering from the most humiliating series of defeats at the hands of the Boers. "Black Week" they called the time when three British generals were beaten in hardly more than six days, plunging England into gloomy consternation. The queen wrote to her prime minister: "Please understand that there is no one depressed in this house. We are not interested in the possibilities of defeat. They do not exist." That other great apostle of courage in adversity, Winston Churchill, said that he thought it was "very sporting of the Boers to take on the whole British empire." The fact that the Boers had been armed by Germany did nothing to moderate Anglo-German hostility; even the speed with which the kaiser hurried to the funeral of his grandmother, Queen Victoria, and his obvious distress on the occasion, failed to modify the ill feeling for "Kaiser Bill."

Then, the violation of Belgian neutrality in 1914 and German references to the violated treaty as a "scrap of paper" brought that ill feeling to a crescendo of hatred and mockery. With his turned-up mustache and his sabre rattling the kaiser seemed to personify Prussian arrogance. The achievement of Wilhelm II was really remarkable, for in a matter of months he created an antagonism in the English people such as Adolf Hitler was unable to create in years. It was an old story, the story of Britain's vital interest in the independence of Belgium, but to the average Englishman it was a moral issue—the breaking of Germany's pledged word. When Neville Chamberlain told the people of Britain that they were at war with Germany again in September, 1939, he could not have done it more effectively than by speaking of the enemy as men of "bad faith." The decline of public morality by our own time may be measured by the fact that hardly anyone would think of speaking in such terms today.

The impact of the First World War on England was like that of a delayed-action bomb. Not for a surprisingly long time did the country understand the true dimensions of what had happened to it. Until then Englishmen had lived the private life of a people who had always been able to pass through life and hardly notice the existence of the state beyond the post office and the policeman. Now the mass of the people became, for the first time, active citizens. As historian A.J.P. Taylor reminds us, they even got up an hour earlier in summer, thanks to an act of parliament in 1916 known as the Daylight Saving Act. It had never before been imagined that Englishmen could be got out of bed by an act of parliament. Hilaire Belloc's famous book *The Servile State* about an England enslaved by legislation had been out nearly five years. As A.J.P. Taylor put it, "the state established a hold over its citizens which, though relaxed in peacetime, was never to be removed, and which the Second World War was to increase. The history of the state and of the English people merged for the first time."

Hegel and other foreign observers had said a century before that the English had no state but only civil society, and apart from some intellectuals like Matthew Arnold most Englishmen believed that and applauded it. During the First World War, however, it was beginning to look as if this happy state of affairs was coming to an end. This was because, as we have learned increasingly in the twentieth century, the

*Kaiser Wilhelm II (left) and his cousin King George V review German troops at Potsdam in 1913, at the last meeting of the two monarchs.*

successful prosecution of a war with a highly organized state requires the opposing state also to become highly organized; at least in this the combatants become more alike. No better example of this could be found than the way England patterned herself increasingly on the model of modern Germany in order to fight the enemy successfully. Even before the two peoples came to blows, Bismarck had invented the welfare state, and it was to Germany that David Lloyd George looked for the model of his social insurance scheme of 1909. The poor quality, both physical and mental, of men conscripted for the armed forces in the First World War set England to thinking further along the lines of legislative action to improve the mental and physical health of her children. Many have gone so far as to say that the welfare state is the child of the warfare state.

By 1914 there existed a minimal amount of legislation on the hours and the places of employment of women and children, although it was still supposed that adult males could and should take care of themselves. After 1909 there were small pensions for the needy over seventy, and after 1911 sickness and unemployment benefits (on a contributory basis) for certain categories of workers. If a man drew such benefits he was said by his mates to have "gone of Lloyd George," a tribute to the man—later prime minister—who had carried through the National Insurance Bill in 1916, an infallible guarantee of immortality.

It was, however, the Second World War that made all the difference in the lives of the English people as dependents of the state. Regimentation was required in order to mount the war effort to defeat the most highly organized people in Europe. The First World War was nothing like "total" in the sense that it came home to the ordinary citizen; in the Second World War aerial bombardment literally brought war home to people. Almost any village war memorial reveals the difference between a war fought by the whole nation and one fought by the "armed forces of the Crown." The distinction between combatant and noncombatant largely disappeared in the Second World War, just as county cricket teams ceased to distinguish between "gentlemen" and "players." Everyone now became a player. As an ancient society whose roots had been for many centuries aristocratic, the English had tended to cling longer than most peoples to the cult of the amateur; they went on hoping until very late that modern wars, like older ones, could be fought by volunteers. Not until 1916, halfway through World War I, did they have recourse to conscription, nor did they submit to the rationing of food until the last year, 1918—and then out of concern for the fair sharing of burdens rather than shortage of men and food supplies, although the latter threatened to become acute when the enemy indulged in unrestricted submarine warfare. The sinking of the liner *Lusitania* in 1915 with 128 Americans aboard was what Voltaire would have called less of a crime than a blunder; as in the Second World War, the entry of the United States could not but settle the outcome.

Britain entered the Second World War as she had entered the First (indeed, all previous wars in alliance with Continental powers), by dispatching troops to France. Four divisions went, in no great hurry, for unlike the first great war with Germany this one was not very active in the west at first. These divisions came at once under unrestricted control of General Gamelin, the French supreme commander; the French sent troops over the German frontier while Hitler was preoccupied with Poland, and withdrew them promptly when the Germans opened fire. This was typical of what came to be called the Phony War, which lasted for some six months. Germany had her hands full in the east, and Hitler wished to think that there would be no cause for extreme measures in the west, while the western powers were under the delusion that Germany would quickly crack up out of economic weakness. What largely made them so reluctant to come to extreme measures, of course, was their exaggerated notion of the overwhelming nature of aerial warfare, for no major war had yet been fought in wholesale fashion by flying machines. Within a few minutes of the declaration of war in September, 1939, the air raid sirens went off in London. The fact that no bombardment followed did not for a moment dispel people's horror about what might have happened.

The symbol of the Phony War was the way the French took their position along the Maginot Line. Some British troops shared this garrison duty, although one had the impression that the British "Tommy" spent most of his energies at this time in killing Hitler "with his mouth," as Kipling had described his own favorite activity with regard to President Kruger in the Boer War. Tommy's songs were unbelievably silly, declaring his object to be to "hang out our washing on the Siegfried Line," or advising Hitler to imitate the rabbit and "run,

run, run." Meanwhile Hitler smashed Poland, having previously swallowed Czechoslovakia; then the Germans occupied Denmark and the best ports in Norway. In the beautiful spring days of 1940 ("Hitler's weather" they called these lovely spells), the German dictator launched an overwhelming weight of armor in a lightning attack on France, compelling her to seek an armistice and driving the English forces back to the Channel. There Hitler paused. If he had been able to maintain the impetus of his advance through France and had flung several divisions across the Channel, he would probably have found a virtually disarmed England at his mercy and won the war there and then. However, he lost the initial momentum. The English stood at Dunkirk, nearly nine hundred ships came to the rescue of the Expeditionary Force where it stood with its back to the sea, and the world witnessed the Miracle of Dunkirk. In all, 338,000 men were rescued and brought back to England, among them 140,000 Frenchmen and 20,000 Poles. In this operation the fortunes of war were determined by two forces which had never before been conceived of as elements of victory: the royal air force and the civilian population navigating small boats in coastal waters. Fighter command fought off the enemy overhead, while a few destroyers and swarms of little boats, pleasure steamers, fishing smacks, even ferryboats, brought the army over the narrow seas at a cost of six destroyers and nearly five hundred aircraft. Nothing was more typical of what Thomas Hardy in *The Dynasts* called the strenuous race. Once more, in the words of the Younger Pitt, the British had saved themselves by their exertions, and were on the way to saving Europe by their example. When the transatlantic democracy came to their aid, it was not simply because the Americans knew that it would be their turn next, but also because no English-speaking people could contemplate the departure of so brave a people from the stage of history.

Winston Churchill, who replaced Neville Chamberlain as prime minister in May of 1940, told the English the grim truth. "We have suffered a great defeat," he said. "Now we are alone." This was hardly grateful, or encouraging to the loyal friends and kinsmen of the Commonwealth, but it was unswervingly honest, the kind of quality which —as he well knew—appeals to his countrymen more immediately and deeply than any mealymouthed latterday talk about "strategic with-

*A motion picture camera records the perilous progress of British soldiers on the Somme battlefield in 1916.*

drawal." He bade them take as their watchwords "grim and gay," and when, at the head of a "National" government, he faced the House of Commons, he told them bluntly that he had nothing to offer but "blood, toil, tears, and sweat." He said also that our policy was to wage war by sea, land, and air, with all our might and with all the strength that God can give us, and that our sole aim was victory—"victory at all costs, however long and hard the road might be."

Churchill was half American, and he had all the "guts" and exuberance of a young people. This tended to make him the ready ally of President Franklin Roosevelt who, despite his physical handicaps, brought to bear the same vigor and freshness. At the very moment when England was bracing herself to fight for survival, indeed in the hour of Dunkirk, Churchill was planning victory, and he infected his countrymen with his hope and faith in their ultimate invincibility. In a hundred phrases he spoke for them, as well as to them, bringing to his words the moralistic touch that had never wholly deserted the English since Cromwell and John Milton. "What sort of people do they think we are?" he burst out in furious contempt when it was brought to him that the enemy hoped England might be open to a separate peace. Another quality that made his success as a British war leader certain was the fact that Churchill was a great eccentric. He was not a comic, but one on his own, like no one else, and easy to "take off" by the popular joker in the pub with his slightly inebriated voice and the ghost of a hiccough. Not least in his verbal tricks was his grotesque mispronunciation of foreign, especially German, names. To call the Nazis "Narzees," and to pronounce Gestapo as the "Jest-a-poe" and the battleship *Graf Spee* as if it rhymed with a cup of tea, held up solemn things to ridicule without underrating their full significance. Only Chatham, and possibly Palmerston, ever made the English laugh so loud and long at a powerful enemy. (Chatham, of course, had also made them laugh at himself.)

After survival the long road to victory had to traverse the valley of death, though not of fear. When Hitler failed to win the war in the first months or the first year, it soon became unlikely that he would win it at all—something that men found hard to believe as he launched his air forces at the "unsinkable aircraft carrier off the mainland of Europe," destroying the House of Commons and even damaging Buckingham Palace. The contrast between this war and that of 1914 came home to people most poignantly in this: in World War I, the tragic departures for the battlefield involved men entraining and sailing for France, while in World War II some of the saddest scenes were enacted on railway platforms where thousands of small children entrained from the cities for temporary homes in safer areas elsewhere. More than 30,000 people were killed in the "blitz" and more than half of them in London. "London can take it," was perhaps the proudest boast of the war: the bombing of the city was destructive of human life and much else, but it saved the airfields from which "the few" operated in the Battle of Britain, which commenced in July, 1940. The German *Luftwaffe* was supposed to have lost 185 aircraft on September 15, the date generally given for the British victory. (The fact that the figure was probably less than 60 that day, while the British lost 26, was nevertheless a sufficient disparity to make Hitler postpone invasion of the island.) The great victory brought forth Churchill's unforgettable phrase: "Never in the field of human conflict was so much owed by so many to so few." This he had already called England's "finest hour." He once said he felt certain that England's history in this and all other crises would be justly written because he was engaged in writing it himself. He wrote it as it was made, and he made much of it.

The cult of equality and the abandonment of privilege in the matter of sharing the burdens of war was, as usual, accompanied by the erosion of liberty. The most noticeable form of equality attained was equality between the sexes—the culmination of a movement that had been going on apace since the start of the suffragette movement in the earliest years of the century. Women chained themselves to railings (preferably in sight of the windows of the country's principal politicians). They set fire to churches. One threw herself beneath the hooves of the king's horse at the Derby. Such antics hardly served to prove women's fitness for the suffrage, but they did draw maximum attention to their readiness to sacrifice life and limb for justice. Far more effective was their proof of both willingness and ability to assume the tasks normally shouldered by men in order to release men for the fighting forces; this demonstration made their unequal position at law patently unjust and unreasonable. After 1918 women attained almost absolute equality in theory, though they did not achieve political suffrage on completely equal terms with men until the Sex Disqualification Removal Act of 1919 opened all professions to them, except in the Church of England and the stock exchange.

The movement toward equality of the sexes was part and parcel of the movement toward the general equality of the classes. The latter owed far more to the Second than to the First World War, and more to the advances of socialism in the world at large than to either. As the Second World War drew to its close, the victors came to include Franklin D. Roosevelt's term a "New Deal" increasingly among their war aims. The people of the West told themselves that the war was being fought for democracy and that democracy for the "common man"—that recent invention—meant equality. The people who had won the war must win the peace, it was argued, but in their jubilation they frequently forgot how much of what they wanted had already been secured as a result of the concessionary policies of the nineteenth century. Free, compulsory, elementary education, for example, was in existence before 1914, and since 1902 secondary education had been increasingly extended. State and major scholarships enabled children from poor and not so poor homes in England to attend the universities, which themselves were already increasing in number. By the 1920s an educated democracy had become a distinct possibility. This was the first requisite of a socialist society, and many of the products of the new dispensation certainly were socialists, or at least sympathetic to the labor movement in their politics.

Although it lasted less than twelve months, England had her first Labor government in 1924, and a second Labor government in 1929 was followed by successive "National" governments. Those who had expressed surprise, indeed disbelief, that the English would adjust themselves to socialism evidently knew little of England. Apart from the celebrated English love of fair play (which was what King George V promised the Labor ministers when they came to power), the English will try anything once if it promises a fair deal for the underdog. They had also the advantage of having experienced much ameliorative legislation at the hands of conservative governments during the nineteenth century, and they recalled Burke's advice that early reforms were treaties made with friends while late ones were often terms granted resentfully by enemies. Many English socialists have been men

*Prime Minister Neville Chamberlain on his 71st birthday in 1940*

of aristocratic upbringing, or at any rate men brought up in schools and universities governed by aristocratic traditions. The king himself, notably George V, often had a weakness for Labor politicians, and Labor politicians tended, as Hilaire Belloc said of English people in general, to prefer King George V to Lloyd George I.

The monarchy, however, was always a law unto itself, largely perhaps because it has so plainly and for so long been under law. The king can do no wrong, the English say, because he cannot do anything. This is not quite true, but there can be no doubt that the prevalence of the notion has saved the monarchy from extinction. "Most disappointing," George V is reputed to have said at the time of the general strike in 1926. "They tell me that they haven't yet bashed a policeman." If this is true it would suggest that the king had little idea of what the strike was all about. The general strike was neither an attempt to challenge the government nor to overthrow the constitution; it was a sympathetic strike in support of the coal miners' struggle for a living wage.

Just ten years later, when George V died, his son and successor Edward VIII felt compelled to abdicate because his ministers were not prepared for him to marry an American lady who had divorced two husbands, one of whom was still living. Attitudes toward divorce had become less rigidly unfavorable by that time, but people still expected an outward show of conformity to the conventions of marriage and far more was expected of the royal personage who stood at the head of the British state and the Established Church. Edward VIII could no doubt have contracted a morganatic marriage, but he wished—as he said in a farewell broadcast at his abdication—to be married like anyone else "to the woman I love." He was a popular man, and no doubt had he cared to make a constitutional issue of it, he would have had widespread support. In fact, however, the whole affair blew over quickly after his abdication and the succession of his brother George VI, who with his consort Queen Elizabeth quickly won the respect and affection of the people. Those who imagined that the abdication crisis had injured the British monarchy found their opinion corrected by the great enhancement of its prestige by George VI and his queen living throughout the war among their people in beleaguered London, blitz and all. In the last third of the twentieth century, with a Prince of Wales who lives the life of most young Englishmen in all essentials, there seems

*London relief workers aid victims of an air raid by German V-2 rockets.*

little reason to entertain doubts about the future of the most ancient institution in England.

The two great wars of the twentieth century have transformed the world in which the greater part of English history had been enacted. It was a world which she had played a large part in building, and whose conformation had for long seemed to depend upon her presence. Its disappearance not only left her impoverished and outpaced by the giants who had been her allies, East and West; it left her under the false impression that she owed history an apology for ever having been a great power. England had ceased to give the law to the subcontinent of India and had seen new nations measure themselves alongside her in Africa and the Far East—nations that continued to use her language and the basic concepts of law and politics she had taught them—yet for all her shrunken stature in terms of wealth and power, she remained in some sense immortal.

What the future holds for England is a matter of insight rather than extrapolation. The historian who attempts to perceive it observes certain lines of force that lie beneath the surface of the nation's historic life, and he is unlikely to go far astray so long as he avoids both loss of nerve and superstition. Loss of nerve has rarely been an English defect. As for superstition, there are only two myths that the English have entertained in later days: first is the one that Britain was once a secure and long-established imperial power, and that she has now fallen from greatness through weakness, benevolence, or some other cause or causes. Everyone who can see straight knows that "little England" only grew into Great Britain against her better nature, and came to hate herself for it, as Kipling himself taught her at the last. Second is the myth that she was once the natural workshop of the world, and supinely lost her pre-eminence. If either concept was ever true, it was for but brief moments in the English past, and it is worth being a historian if only to know it. There is, however, one thing that the English past tells us at every moment and with certainty. Her great national poet told his countrymen in the last lines of *King John:*

> *Nought shall make us rue,*
> *If England to itself do rest but true.*

*Winston Churchill leading a party of Allied Command officers as they disembark from a landing craft on the east bank of the Rhine in 1945*

# CHRONOLOGY

| | |
|---|---|
| **1200–300 B.C.** | Invasions by Celtic-speaking peoples |
| **55–54** | Julius Caesar's expedition to Britain |
| **A.D. 5–40** | The Roman conquest of Britain |
| **48–79** | Conquest of Wales; construction of Roman roads |
| **62** | Defeat of Queen Boadicea |
| **313** | Christianity is introduced to Britain |
| **350–597** | Invasions by Angles, Saxons, and Jutes |
| **410–442** | Withdrawal of Roman legions from Britain |
| **597** | Augustine re-establishes the Roman Church |
| **731** | The Venerable Bede's *Ecclesiastical History* |
| **856–875** | Viking raids reach their peak |
| **871–899** | Alfred the Great defeats the Danes |
| **1017–1035** | Canute rules England, Denmark, and Norway |
| **1066** | William the Conqueror wins the Battle of Hastings |
| **1066–1087** | William I centralizes authority of the Crown |
| **1154–1189** | Reign of Henry II (*first ruler of house of Plantagenet*) |
| **1170** | Assassination of Thomas à Becket |
| **1189–1199** | Reign of Richard I, the Lionhearted |
| **1215** | King John signs the Magna Carta at Runnymede |
| **1295** | Edward I convenes his "Model Parliament" |
| **1337** | Edward III claims French throne; Hundred Years' War |
| **1346** | English victory at Crécy |
| **1348–1349** | The Black Death ravages England |
| **1381** | The Peasants' Revolt |
| **1399–1413** | Reign of Henry IV (*first ruler of house of Lancaster*) |
| **1415** | Henry V's victory at the Battle of Agincourt |
| **1455–1485** | The Wars of the Roses, between Lancaster and York |
| **1461–1483** | Reign of Edward IV (*first ruler of house of York*) |
| **1483** | The duke of Gloucester usurps the throne as Richard III |
| **1485** | Richard III's defeat at Bosworth Field; Henry VII (*first ruler of house of Tudor*) is crowned |
| **1534** | The Act of Supremacy; Henry VIII becomes head of the Church of England |
| **1553–1558** | The reign of "Bloody" Mary Tudor restores Catholicism |
| **1559** | Elizabeth I reasserts the Act of Supremacy |
| **1587** | Mary Queen of Scots is beheaded |
| **1588** | England defeats the Invincible Armada |
| **1600** | Charter of the East India Company |
| **1603–1625** | Reign of James I (*first ruler of house of Stuart*) |

| | |
|---|---|
| **1611** | Publication of the King James Bible |
| **1629** | Charles I dissolves parliament |
| **1640–1653** | Convening of the "Long Parliament" |
| **1642–1646** | The civil war between Puritans and parliamentarians ("Roundheads"), and royalists ("Cavaliers") |
| **1649** | Charles I is executed; a Commonwealth is established |
| **1653–1658** | Oliver Cromwell rules over a one-man protectorate |
| **1660** | The restoration of Charles II |
| **1666** | The Great Fire of London |
| **1688–1689** | The "Glorious Revolution"; James II is deposed, and William of Orange and his wife Mary are crowned |
| **1704** | The duke of Marlborough's victory at Blenheim |
| **1707** | England and Scotland unite as "Great Britain" |
| **1714–1727** | Reign of George I (*first ruler of house of Hanover*) |
| **1739–1741** | The War of Jenkin's Ear |
| **1740–1748** | The War of the Austrian Succession |
| **1745** | The second Jacobite rebellion under Charles Stuart |
| **1756–1763** | The Seven Years' War (French and Indian Wars); British sovereignty in North America |
| **1757** | Robert Clive extends British territories in India |
| **1775–1783** | The War of American Independence |
| **1793–1815** | War with Revolutionary France; the Napoleonic Wars |
| **1800** | Great Britain and Ireland unite as the "United Kingdom" |
| **1812–1815** | War with the United States (the War of 1812) |
| **1815** | Wellington defeats Napoleon at Waterloo |
| **1822–1846** | Period of parliamentary reforms and social legislation |
| **1837–1901** | Reign of Queen Victoria |
| **1839–1842** | The Opium War; annexation of Hong Kong |
| **1846** | Robert Peel repeals the Corn Laws |
| **1851** | The Great Exhibition at the Crystal Palace |
| **1854–1856** | Britain fights Turkey in the Crimean War |
| **1875** | The British control the Suez Canal |
| **1880s–1890s** | Cecil Rhodes annexes African territory |
| **1899–1902** | The Boer War |
| **1905–1914** | Era of Liberal reform under David Lloyd George |
| **1914–1919** | The First World War |
| **1919–1922** | Ireland wins Home Rule as the Irish Free State |
| **1936** | Edward VIII abdicates |
| **1939–1945** | The Second World War |
| **1940** | Winston Churchill elected prime minister |
| **1940** | The RAF wins the Battle of Britain |
| **1947** | India and Pakistan achieve commonwealth status |
| **1951** | Churchill returns to power |
| **1952** | Accession of Elizabeth II |

# CREDITS AND INDEX

**2** Base map drawn by Richard Edes Harrison, courtesy of Ginn and Company, A Xerox Company, Lexington, Mass. **6** Herschel Levit **10–11** Ministry of Public Building and Works. Crown Copyright **13** Metropolitan Museum of Art **17** Trinity College Library, Dublin **18** Norwegian Information Service, New York **21** Bibliothèque Nationale **22 top** Courtesy of the Trustees of the British Musuem **22 bot.** Kloster Engelberg **24** British Travel and Holidays Association, London **28–29** Bayeux tapestry, by permission of the city of Bayeux; Giraudon **31** A.C. Bouquet, *European Brasses,* London, 1967 **34** Courtesy of the Trustees of the British Museum **39** Collection of Kofler-Truniger, Lucerne **41** Bibliothèque Nationale **44** Conzett and Huber–Franco Gianetti **49** Warden and Fellows of New College, Oxford **50** Gernsheim Collection, University of Texas, Austin **52** Musée de l'Arsenal, Paris **58–59** Courtesy of the Trustees of the British Museum **61** Treasurer and Masters of the Bench of the Inner Temple, London **62 both** Courtesy of the Trustees of the British Museum **64–65** Henry E. Huntington Library and Gallery, San Marino, Calif. **68** Herschel Levit **72** Walker Art Gallery, Liverpool, England **75** Courtesy of the Trustees of the Goodwood Collection **78** National Galleries of Scotland **81** National Portrait Gallery, London **82** Courtesy of the Trustees of the British Museum **86–87** Mrs. Catherine Palmer **89** Courtesy of the Trustees of the British Museum **90** *Country Life* Magazine **93** New York Public Library **95** Metropolitan Museum of Art **96** Louvre **100–101** Scottish National Portrait Gallery **105** Mansell Collection **108** A.F. Kersting **113** Science Museum, London **114** Royal Society, London **116–17** London Museum **119** Mauritshuis, The Hague **121** Victoria and Albert Museum. Crown Copyright **122–23** Aerofilms and Aero Pictorial Ltd., London **126** Collection of the Marquess of Cholmondeley **129, 130** Courtesy of the Trustees of the British Museum **132** British Travel and Holiday Association, London **137, 138** Courtesy of the Trustees of the British Museum **141** National Portrait Gallery, London **144** National Gallery of Canada **147** John Carter Brown Library, Brown University, Providence **148–49** Richard Paton, USNAM **151** Metropolitan Museum of Art **152** New York Public Library **154** Thames and Hudson–Edwin Smith **156** National Gallery, London **159** Royal College of Surgeons' Museum, London **160–61** Walker Art Gallery, Liverpool, England **164 top** R. Ackermann, *Microcosm of London,* London, 1808–1811 **164 bot.** New York Public Library **167 top** National Maritime Museum, Greenwich, England **167 bot.** Metropolitan Museum of Art **170** National Maritime Museum, Greenwich, England **174** Photo Researchers **177** Bibliothèque Nationale **181** R. Ackermann, *Microcosm of London,* London, 1801–1811 **184** New York Public Library **186** Radio Times Hulton Picture Library **189** Courtesy of the Trustees of the British Museum **190–91** Thomas Daniel, *Oriental Survey,* London, 1795–1807 **193** National Portrait Gallery, London **194** Library of Congress **198** Photo Researchers **202–203** Imperial War Museum, London **205** Press Association, Ltd., London **208** Imperial War Museum, London **213** Radio Times Hulton Picture Library **214** *LIFE* Magazine © Time Inc.–George Rogers **216** Imperial War Museum, London

Page numbers in **boldface type** refer to illustrations.
Page references to map entries are in *italic type.*